"How I rejoice to see thinkers of Stephen Nichols's caliber applying their fine minds to the life and thought of the inimitable Dietrich Bonhoeffer. There's so much yet to be written about this great man. A hungry readership awaits!"

Eric Metaxas, *New York Times* best-selling author, *Bonhoeffer: Pastor, Martyr, Prophet, Spy*

"This book will quicken your pulse as you are drawn into the story and the example of Dietrich Bonhoeffer. Stephen Nichols brings a long and complex life to a point of ongoing personal application. This book prompted me to pray for the kind of courage that comes only after intense communion with the living God. Read and be strengthened."

Russell D. Moore, President, the Southern Baptist Ethics & Religious Liberty Commission

"'Human weakness paves the way for God's grace.' So writes Stephen Nichols, using Dietrich Bonhoeffer as a guide to the Christian life. But how could a man who stood up to Hitler be considered weak? That's what makes Bonhoeffer so fascinating, and why he deserves your attention. Nichols helpfully brings Bonhoeffer's Christ-centered insights to bear on issues where we need to grow in grace, such as confession, freedom, and love."

Collin Hansen, Editorial Director, The Gospel Coalition; coauthor, *A God-Sized Vision: Revival Stories That Stretch and Stir*

"Bonhoeffer was a unique man who understood the power of both conviction and compassion, clarity and ambiguity, narrative and poetry. Through this man the church is powerfully reminded that all theology is *lived* theology. In this book, Steve Nichols takes us into Bonhoeffer's complex world and offers a rich set of reflections on such crucial themes as cross, community, and the living Word. Here the reader discovers a wonderful mixture of fair-minded historical reconstruction and wise pastoral counsel."

Kelly M. Kapic, Professor of Theological Studies, Covenant College

"Dietrich Bonhoeffer's life illustrates the truth that God's power is made perfect in our weakness. His courageous stand against the Nazi regime is a powerful testament to his cross-centered theology and belief that weakness is the starting point for Christian spirituality. With insight, clarity, and wisdom, Stephen Nichols guides us through the life and work of this humble yet heroic pastor, whose example shows that all Christian living flows from God's grace in the cross of Christ."

Justin Holcomb, Executive Director, Resurgence; author, *On the Grace of God*

D1373867

BONHOEFFER

on the Christian Life

THEOLOGIANS ON THE CHRISTIAN LIFE

EDITED BY STEPHEN J. NICHOLS AND JUSTIN TAYLOR

Schaeffer on the Christian Life:
Countercultural Spirituality,
William Edgar

Warfield on the Christian Life:
Living in Light of the Gospel,
Fred G. Zaspel

BONHOEFFER

on the Christian Life

FROM THE CROSS, FOR THE WORLD

STEPHEN J. NICHOLS

WHEATON, ILLINOIS

Cover design: Josh Dennis
Cover image: Richard Solomon Artists, Mark Summers

First printing 2013
Printed in the United States of America

The author's Scripture quotations are from the ESV® Bible (*The Holy Bible, English Standard Version®*), copyright © 2001 by Crossway. 2011 Text Edition. Used by permission. All rights reserved.

Scripture marked KJV is from the King James Version of the Bible.

Trade paperback ISBN: 978-1-4335-1188-2
Mobipocket ISBN: 978-1-4335-1190-5
PDF ISBN: 978-1-4335-1189-2
ePub ISBN: 978-1-4335-2398-4

Library of Congress Cataloging-in-Publication Data

Nichols, Stephen J., 1970–
  Bonhoeffer on the Christian life : from the cross, for the world / Stephen J. Nichols.
      pages cm. — (Theologians on the Christian life)
    Includes bibliographical references and index.
    ISBN 978-1-4335-1188-2 (tp)
    1. Bonhoeffer, Dietrich, 1906–1945. I. Title.
  BX4827.B57N525   2013
  230'.044092—dc23   2013000954

Crossway is a publishing ministry of Good News Publishers.

VP		23	22	21	20	19	18	17	16	15	14	13
15	14	13	12	11	10	9	8	7	6	5	4	3	2	1

To Allan Fisher
in honor of his decades of service in Christian publishing
and in gratitude for his friendship

CONTENTS

SERIES PREFACE

Some might call us spoiled. We live in an era of significant and substantial resources for Christians on living the Christian life. We have ready access to books, DVD series, online material, seminars—all in the interest of encouraging us in our daily walk with Christ. The laity, the people in the pew, have access to more information than scholars dreamed of having in previous centuries.

Yet for all our abundance of resources, we also lack something. We tend to lack the perspectives from the past, perspectives from a different time and place than our own. To put the matter differently, we have so many riches in our current horizon that we tend not to look to the horizons of the past.

That is unfortunate, especially when it comes to learning about and practicing discipleship. It's like owning a mansion and choosing to live in only one room. This series invites you to explore the other rooms.

As we go exploring, we will visit places and times different from our own. We will see different models, approaches, and emphases. This series does not intend for these models to be copied uncritically, and it certainly does not intend to put these figures from the past high upon a pedestal like some race of super-Christians. This series intends, however, to help us in the present listen to the past. We believe there is wisdom in the past twenty centuries of the church, wisdom for living the Christian life.

Stephen J. Nichols and Justin Taylor

ACKNOWLEDGMENTS

Book buyers incur debts. So too book writers. As the writer of this one, I gladly take on much debt of gratitude. I am thankful for my friends who helped me either directly or indirectly with this book, including Keith Krueger, Tim Larsen, Chris Larson, Sean Lucas, and Jeff Trimbath. I am also thankful to Dale Mort, who read through an earlier manuscript and offered most helpful comments and corrections.

I remain indebted to the community of Lancaster Bible College for generously supporting my work. Thanks especially to Drs. Peter Teague and Philip Dearborn for unflagging encouragement. My students also deserve a word of thanks for allowing me, even if involuntarily, to interject Bonhoeffer into nearly every class for the last three years. Two students in particular, Michael Bauer and Andrew Keenan, read through the final stages of the manuscript. Thank you both.

Thom Notaro at Crossway proved an astute and careful editor. And there's Justin Taylor, coeditor of this series and a most valued friend. Working on this series with you, Justin, and on this book in particular, has been a delight. I am much in your debt, again.

I also remain in debt to my family. They keep all these book-related things in perspective. To Heidi especially, thank you.

Finally, I need to start paying on the debt I owe to Allan Fisher. For decades, Al has been a fixture in the Christian publishing world, first at Baker, then at P&R, and for the last eight years at Crossway. Al welcomed me into this business and so graciously helped me along every step of the journey for these past dozen years that I have been writing. I and so many authors and readers are in his debt. Bonhoeffer once spoke of our inability to express ourselves at certain moments, saying "all desire for great words fades away." So let me simply say to you, Al, thank you.

ABBREVIATIONS

DBWE 1   *Dietrich Bonhoeffer Works*, English edition. Vol. 1,
          Sanctorum Communio

DBWE 2   *Dietrich Bonhoeffer Works*, English edition. Vol. 2,
          Act and Being

DBWE 3   *Dietrich Bonhoeffer Works*, English edition. Vol. 3,
          Creation and Fall

DBWE 4   *Dietrich Bonhoeffer Works*, English edition. Vol. 4,
          Discipleship

DBWE 5   *Dietrich Bonhoeffer Works*, English edition. Vol. 5,
          Life Together and *Prayerbook of the Bible*

DBWE 6   *Dietrich Bonhoeffer Works*, English edition. Vol. 6,
          Ethics

DBWE 7   *Dietrich Bonhoeffer Works*, English edition. Vol. 7,
          Fiction from Tegel Prison

DBWE 8   *Dietrich Bonhoeffer Works*, English edition. Vol. 8,
          Letters and Papers from Prison

DBWE 9   *Dietrich Bonhoeffer Works*, English edition. Vol. 9,
          The Young Bonhoeffer: 1918–1927

DBWE 10   *Dietrich Bonhoeffer Works*, English edition. Vol. 10,
          Barcelona, Berlin, New York: 1928–1931

DBWE 11   *Dietrich Bonhoeffer Works*, English edition. Vol. 11,
          Ecumenical, Academic, and Pastoral Work: 1931–1932

DBWE 12   *Dietrich Bonhoeffer Works*, English edition. Vol. 12,
          Berlin: 1932–1933

DBWE 13   *Dietrich Bonhoeffer Works*, English edition. Vol. 13,
          London: 1933–1935

DBWE 15   *Dietrich Bonhoeffer Works*, English edition. Vol. 15,
          Theological Education Underground: 1937–1940

DBWE 16   *Dietrich Bonhoeffer Works*, English edition. Vol. 16,
              Conspiracy and Imprisonment: 1940–1945

     LPP   Dietrich Bonhoeffer, *Letters and Papers from Prison*,
              Enlarged edition. Edited by Eberhard Bethge. New York:
              Simon & Schuster, 1997.

      LT   Dietrich Bonhoeffer, *Life Together*. Translated by Jon W.
              Doberstein. San Francisco: Harper, 1954.

Note: The *Dietrich Bonhoeffer Works*, English edition, all published by Fortress Press, Minneapolis, are translations of the sixteen-volume set, *Dietrich Bonhoeffer Werke*, ed. Eberhard Bethge et al. (Munich: Christian Kaiser Verlag, 1986–1999).

PART I

INTRODUCTION

Today I'm supposed to learn how to play golf.

DIETRICH BONHOEFFER
TO HIS BROTHER KARL-FRIEDRICH BONHOEFFER,
FROM PHILADELPHIA, 1930

CHAPTER I

MEETING BONHOEFFER

I believe that nothing meaningless has happened to me and also that it is good for us when things run counter to our desires. I see a purpose in my present existence and only hope that I fulfill it.

DIETRICH BONHOEFFER[1]

On a hot summer's day in July 1939, Dietrich Bonhoeffer stepped off the steamship *Bremen* and onto the docks of New York City's harbor. The harbor was busy that year. New York City was playing host to the World's Fair, an event altogether eclipsed by the tensions of the pending world war. By September, a United States Navy fleet had moved in to protect the harbor, and mines had been placed along the coast in fear of a German submarine attack. Bonhoeffer knew all too well the tension. He had lived with much worse for some time and was now on his way to America to escape.

Bonhoeffer had been to the United States before. His first trip had come nine years earlier. Already with a doctorate in hand, Bonhoeffer thought he might benefit from studying American theological developments firsthand before settling in to his faculty position at Berlin. So off he went to spend a year at Union Seminary in New York. During that first stay, he had forged deep friendships. One of those friends, Reinhold Niebuhr of Union's faculty, now led the way in arranging for Bonhoeffer's second trip to America. Niebuhr hurriedly posted letters to his academic colleagues throughout

---

[1] Quoted in Renate Bethge, *Dietrich Bonhoeffer: A Brief Life* (Minneapolis: Fortress, 2004), 68.

America to cobble together a lecture tour for Bonhoeffer, in part to fund his stay and in part to shake out a more substantial and permanent teaching offer. At thirty-three years of age and with an impressive list of accomplishments already, Bonhoeffer had a bright career ahead of him.

Bonhoeffer, though, would elude Niebuhr's efforts. The moment Bonhoeffer stepped off the ship, he knew that he had made a mistake. He belonged back in Germany. His diary bears the record, "The decision has been made."[2] "I have made a mistake in coming to America," he wrote to Niebuhr. "I must live through this difficult period in our national history with the Christian people of Germany."[3] To their mutual friend Paul Lehmann, Bonhoeffer wrote, "I must be with my brothers when things become serious."[4]

Bonhoeffer anticipated that Germany would survive the war. He also realized that the German church, like the nation itself, would need to be rebuilt. After all, how could he play a role in rebuilding the church if he abandoned it during its hour of deepest need? No, he could not stay in America.

Writing to Lehmann, Niebuhr could only say of Bonhoeffer's decision, "I do not understand it all."[5] Who can understand Bonhoeffer's decision? What kind of person would be more at ease in facing down a totalitarian regime on the brink of destruction than conducting a college lecture tour in a free and democratic society an ocean away from the tumult and wreckage of war? What's more, this was no isolated decision, no adrenaline-charged heroism. Dietrich Bonhoeffer's willingness to return to Germany, his willingness to face Hitler and the Nazi regime, ultimately his willingness to die, all stemmed from a deeply honed reflex. He could no more walk away from Germany in 1939—when he had opportunity to do so—than you or I can stop our hearts from beating. To understand Bonhoeffer's decision in the dog days of a New York summer of 1939, you need to understand Bonhoeffer.

We should not take this episode as evidence of Bonhoeffer's heroism. The impulse is understandable, even tempting, but would be a misunderstanding. The letters and his diary point in an entirely different direction. This was no act of blazoned courage. Rather, his decision reveals a brash faith. See him as humble, not heroic. See him as dependent upon God. As he writes in his diary, "God certainly sees how much personal concern, how much fear is contained in today's decision, as courageous as it may appear.

[2] Bonhoeffer, "American Diary," June 20, 1939, DBWE 15:226. His entry on the following day reveals that he resolved the struggle over the decision by ultimately conceding, "God knows" (229).
[3] Bonhoeffer to Reinhold Niebuhr, during the end of June 1939, DBWE 15:210.
[4] Bonhoeffer to Paul Lehmann, June 30, 1939, DBWE 15:209.
[5] Reinhold Niebuhr to Paul Lehmann, July 8, 1939, DBWE 15:216.

. . . At the end of the day, I can only pray that God may hold merciful judgment over this day and all decisions. It is now in God's hands."[6] If we flip
back a few pages to earlier in his American diary, we see that being in God's
hands means being a recipient of God's mercy through and in Christ. The
opening pages of his American diary bear the testimony, "Only when we
ourselves live and speak entirely from the mercy of Christ and no longer at
all out of our own particular knowledge and experience, then we will not
be sanctimonious."[7]

To understand Bonhoeffer, we must understand, on the one hand, the
limits of oneself and, on the other hand, the utter absence of limits of God.
Bonhoeffer saw himself as limited in his understanding, limited in his experience, limited in his resolve, limited in his strength. To trust in himself
would be purely—and merely—sanctimony, the religion of Pharisees. But
to trust in God would be altogether different. To understand Bonhoeffer, we
must first and foremost understand living by faith.

Dietrich Bonhoeffer once wrote that to live by faith (he would say to live
truly) means "living unreservedly in life's duties, problems, successes and
failures, experiences and perplexities."[8] He wrote of the great cost of cheap
grace to the church and its disciples in the modern world. He saw far too
many examples of a culturally accommodated and culturally captive Christianity. He longed for a costly discipleship. So he compelled the church and
its disciples to consider costly grace, to consider the cost of discipleship.
Costly discipleship is held captive to Christ; it is Christ-centered. He might
have even coined a German word to express this, *Christuswirklichkeit*, a
living in the one realm of the Christ reality.[9] Bonhoeffer also wrote per-
suasively of how this Christ-centered or Christ-reality living is the "life together," the life of community, centered on our common union with Christ.
No, we are not individual heroes achieving greatness—an unfortunate but
prevalent model of living the Christian life in our day. Instead, we live together in Christ by faith.

Understanding Bonhoeffer, however, entails more than seeing this life
of faith in Christ theologically. It also involves seeing how this theological
center manifests itself in his life, in his daily comings and goings. Bonhoeffer was a theologian and a churchman, but he was also a person.

---

[6] Bonhoeffer, "American Diary," June 20, 1939, *DBWE* 15:227.
[7] Bonhoeffer, "American Diary," June 8, 1939, *DBWE* 15:217.
[8] Bonhoeffer to Eberhard Bethge, July 21, 1944, *LPP*, 370.
[9] *DBWE* 6:58.

Bonhoeffer wrote poems, for example:

Distant or near,
in joy or in sorrow,
each in the other
sees his true helper
to brotherly freedom.[10]

He tried his hand at a novel. He had a twin sister. He was, for a time, a youth pastor who could play the guitar. He frequented the theater, knew his way around an art gallery. He had opinions on art, music, and architecture. "You're quite right," he wrote from his prison cell, "about the rarity of landscape painting in the South generally. Is the south of France an exception—and Gauguin?"[11] He was a professor of theology at the University of Berlin. He took on a rather rough band of youth on a different side of the tracks from which he had come of age. He prepared them for their first communion and, when the time had come for it, bought them all new suits for the occasion.

Bonhoeffer led an underground seminary, often looking out the window during his early afternoon lectures. On more than one day, with sun shining and a cool breeze gently bending tree limbs, he would grab a soccer ball on his way out the door and his students would fall in behind.

He was a spy. He helped Jews escape from the Nazis. He became part of a ring of conspirators in plots to assassinate Hitler.

He became engaged to Maria von Wedemeyer in January 1943, and three months later he was imprisoned at Tegel. During the fall months of 1944, he was transferred to the Gestapo prison in Berlin. He spent the final weeks of his life listening to sirens signaling the incessant dropping of bombs while cut off from his books, paper, pens, and ink.

He was a martyr.

Dietrich Bonhoeffer, both in his life and in his writings, draws us in. He demands our attention—not like the tantrums of a two-year-old, but like the quiet, trusted voice of a wise friend. That voice of Bonhoeffer's, though quiet, has never been silent. A century after his birth, it resounds with clarity and grace. Historian and biographer David McCullough has said, "We are shaped by those we never met." That's quite true—or at least it should be.

---

[10] Bonhoeffer, "The Friend," c. August, 1944, *LPP*, 390.
[11] Bonhoeffer to Eberhard Bethge, March 25, 1944, *LPP*, 239.

Perhaps Bonhoeffer shapes us best by showing us in word and in deed, as a theologian and in his life, how to live the Christian life, how to be a disciple of Christ, how to live in the *Christuswirklichkeit*. His book *The Cost of Discipleship* gets all of the attention on this score, and rightfully so. *The Cost of Discipleship* would be a legacy in and of itself. But Bonhoeffer offers us more. We owe it to ourselves, as well as to the honor of his memory, to widen our attention. This present book on Bonhoeffer on the Christian life proposes to do just that.

From *The Cost of Discipleship* we learn of the difference between a Christianity that asks nothing of us and one that requires a 180-degree turn from all that comes naturally. We learn of the difference between cheap grace and costly grace.

From *Life Together* and from his doctoral thesis, *Sanctorum Communio* (*The Communion of Saints*), written as he was not yet twenty-one, we learn that the Christian life is lived both alone and together. It is the together part that can be a challenge for us. It is also the together part that has become in our day the buzzword of community.

For Bonhoeffer, community was more than a trendy word; it was his life. In *Letters and Papers from Prison*, edited by Eberhard Bethge and published posthumously, Bonhoeffer teaches us that "it is only by living completely in this world that one learns to have faith," words he wrote while living in a six-by-nine-foot prison cell.[12] We also learn from his unfinished and unpublished novel, written during his imprisonment, about the true nature and task and mission of the church. Academic books, like his unfinished magnum opus *Ethics*, as well as his numerous essays, lectures, sermons, and even his diaries and scribbled-down rough thoughts from his imprisonment, round out what Bonhoeffer has to offer us in words.

As for what Bonhoeffer offers us in deeds, both in his life and in his death he shows us how to love and serve God. Like Paul, Bonhoeffer knew firsthand both extremes of plenty and of want (Phil. 4:12). Growing up he enjoyed the life of moderate wealth. Childhood was punctuated with long vacations at the summer home, governesses, and family oratorios performed in their very own conservatory, which doubled as the family parlor. He started his academic career at the prestigious University of Berlin.

---

[12] *LPP*, 369.

But along came Hitler. Bonhoeffer lost his license to teach, and he traded in Berlin for Finkenwalde. Yes, Finkenwalde was an estate, but better to think run-down monastery than paneled walls and luxurious rooms. And then he was sent to prison. While in prison he once wrote of his longing to hear birds and see color. He knew all too well what it meant to be in want.

> Or am I only what I know of myself,
> restless and longing and sick, like a bird in a cage,
> struggling for breath, as though hands were compressing my throat,
> yearning for colors, for flowers, for the voices of birds,
> thirsting for words of kindness, for neighborliness.[13]

And, like Paul, these experiences of plenty and want led Bonhoeffer to contentment. He expressed this in a poem marking the occasion of the New Year in 1945. Bonhoeffer had spent the whole of 1944 in Nazi prisons. "The old year," he writes of 1944, "still torments our hearts."[14] By December he was in Berlin, and his precious flow of letters and books in and out had been cut to a mere trickle.

In one of those rare letters, allowed to be sent to his mother on her birthday, he tucked in his New Year's poem entitled "The Powers of Good."

> Should it be ours to drain the cup of grieving
> even to the dregs of pain, at thy command,
> we will not falter, thankfully receiving
> all that is given by thy loving hand.
>
> But should it be thy will once more to release us
> to life's enjoyment and its good sunshine,
> that which we've learned from sorrow shall increase us,
> and all our life be dedicated as thine.[15]

It was Christ who gave us the ultimate paradox of life: in the keeping of our life we lose it, but in the giving of our life we find it (Matt. 10:39). Christ spoke these words immediately on the heels of telling his disciples to take up their cross (10:38). From the very beginning that has been the call to discipleship, the call to live the Christian life. Bonhoeffer, as well as or if

---

[13] Bonhoeffer, "Who Am I?," c. July 1944, *LPP*, 348.
[14] *LPP*, 400.
[15] *LPP*, 400.

not better than any other person in the twentieth century, understood this and lived it, both in darkest night and in the full light of the sun. He understood what it meant to be unreservedly dedicated to Christ, to live by faith.

Consequently, Bonhoeffer deserves a place among theologians of the past who can serve as guides for us in the present for living the Christian life. He literally wrote the book on discipleship, but he also, as mentioned above, has more to offer than his classic text *The Cost of Discipleship*. He *lived* discipleship. An old Carter family song croons, "It takes a worried man to sing a worried song." I think that means authenticity matters. And the stakes regarding authenticity could not be higher than when it comes to discipleship. This lyric from the Carter song also means you can spot a fake. And Bonhoeffer was no imposter. He was a disciple, so he could well sing—and preach and write—of discipleship.

In our current day we have more material on living the Christian life—in the form of books, seminars, conferences, and DVDs—than at any other time in the history of the church. Much of that material focuses on the individual, on our personal prayer life and our private devotional time. Much of that material also focuses on duty—the roll-up-your-sleeves, get-it-done-by-grit-and-determination approach. Further still, much of this talk of spirituality also sounds rather otherworldly, disconnected from the twists and turns of daily life. Rodney Clapp writes of this otherworldly emphasis as resulting in a spirituality for angels, not for flesh-and-blood humans.[16] Especially in the context of North American evangelicalism, we tend to define living the Christian life and spirituality along these individualistic, works- or performance-oriented, and detached/otherworldly lines. More often than not, following these kinds of approaches to discipleship leaves us defeated and discouraged. Humans have a hard time performing on the level of angels.

While Bonhoeffer does speak of the personal spiritual disciplines, the "life alone" as he calls it, he also speaks of the "life together," reminding us of our union with Christ and the common union we share with one another in the body of Christ, the church. While Bonhoeffer does speak of duty, he also heralds grace. He is, after all, a Lutheran, so he knows a thing or two about grace. Finally, while Bonhoeffer does speak of the life to come, his is a "worldly discipleship," deeply connected to the ups and downs of life in this fallen world. This voice from the past can help us avoid missteps on

---

[16] Rodney Clapp, *Tortured Wonders: Christian Spirituality for People, Not Angels* (Grand Rapids: Brazos, 2006).

our walk with Christ in the present. We owe it to ourselves to meet him and to listen to what he has to say—both in word and in deed.

———————

We will begin our explorations of all that Bonhoeffer has to offer fellow disciples by looking at the foundations of the Christian life. He commends to us the cross-centered life. Bonhoeffer scholars speak of "Christo-ecclesiology" as the center of Bonhoeffer's thought, which is to say that Bonhoeffer has both christology (the doctrine of Christ) and ecclesiology (the doctrine of the church) at the center of his theology, like the hub of a wheel. It might even be better to say that Bonhoeffer's ecclesiology flows from, naturally and necessarily, his christology. So we start with Bonhoeffer's *christology* (chap. 2) and then move to Bonhoeffer's *ecclesiology* (chap. 3).

Bonhoeffer takes a page from his favorite theologian, Martin Luther. For Luther, too, Christ is at the center. And at the center of the center is Christ on the cross. Early on and then throughout his life Luther spoke of a theology of the cross, as does Bonhoeffer. So theology, Christian living—all of reality—flows from the cross.

This life from the cross (Bonhoeffer's christology) and life in the church (his ecclesiology) together lead to the disciplines of the Christian life. We will explore three of them: reading and obeying Scripture, prayer, and the practice of theology. I have chosen these three because Bonhoeffer, speaking in the context of the underground seminary he led in the late 1930s, saw this trilogy of disciplines as the essential ingredients for a ministerial education. He desired only that his students knew how to read *and did read* the Bible, that they knew how to *and did* pray, and that they both thought *and lived* theologically. For him seminary was about imparting knowledge (referred to as *scientia* by the ancients) and about spiritual formation and life (referred to as *formation* by the ancients). And this illustrates that what's good for the goose is indeed good for the gander. In other words, what's good for ministers is good for all of us. These three are the essential practices of the Christian life, and all of them constitute worship.

In chapter 4, we will see Bonhoeffer's *doctrine of Scripture*—a significant item in the debate over whether Bonhoeffer was a conservative, even evangelical, theologian or a liberal theologian. But we will also explore Bonhoeffer's own practice of reading Scripture and what we stand to learn from it. Next comes *prayer* (chap. 5), paradoxically the easiest but also the hardest discipline of the Christian life. Finally, we look at the role of *thinking theologically and then living theologically* (chap. 6). Theology sometimes gets pitted against Christian life. One is theory, the other practice. Bonhoeffer will help us see the unity of the two and not fall prey to a deadly divide.

This life from the cross not only leads to these three disciplines of Scripture, prayer, and theology but also leads us out into the world. We would better say that it leads us to live for the world. The final three chapters explore what this means by looking first at Bonhoeffer's curious but delightful phrase "worldly Christianity." *Worldliness* (chap. 7) is something we should avoid—after all, we are not "of the world," and we should not be "conformed to the world" (John 15:19; Rom. 12:2)—but we first need to listen carefully to what Bonhoeffer really means. Next comes *freedom*, camouflaged as *service* and *sacrifice*, as chapter 8 looks at Bonhoeffer's spirit of service and the call to sacrifice. The classic text on living the Christian life, Romans 12:1–2, calls us to be living sacrifices. For Bonhoeffer this first entailed sacrificing his position as he lost his post at Berlin, then sacrificing his freedom as he was imprisoned, and then sacrificing his life as he was hanged at Flossenbürg Concentration Camp on April 9, 1945.

But his death should not have the final word. That goes to *love*, the subject of chapter 9. All of this—the service, the sacrifices, the worldliness, the Scripture reading, prayer, and practice of theology, that is, the life in community and the life from the cross—all of it is accentuated by love. Jesus laid down this characteristic as the hallmark of discipleship and of the church (John 13:34–35). Bonhoeffer called it the "extraordinary."

Dietrich Bonhoeffer died in his thirty-ninth year, a time when most people are just beginning to faintly understand life. He was, however, a quick study. Some of that had to do with circumstance, the utterly harsh and despicable experiences he endured. Think of the remarkable insight of the so young Anne Frank. Challenging circumstances can lead people into profound depths of understanding, no matter what their age. But in Bonhoeffer's case not all such depths can be chalked up to his mere experiences. Bonhoeffer so well understood how to live because he so well understood the cross on which Christ died. Bonhoeffer also grasped the all-encompassing implications of the cross for human existence. He lived from the cross for the world. This is why he's worth meeting.

PART 2

FOUNDATIONS

What is the "extraordinary"? It is the love of Jesus Christ himself, who goes to the cross in suffering and obedience. It is the cross. What is unique in Christianity is the cross.

DIETRICH BONHOEFFER,
THE COST OF DISCIPLESHIP, 1937

I think we're going to have an exceptionally good Christmas. The very fact that every outward circumstance precludes our making provision for it will show whether we can be content with what is truly essential. I used to be very fond of thinking up and buying presents, but now that we have nothing to give, the gift God gave us in the birth of Christ will seem all the more glorious; the emptier our hands, the better we understand what Luther meant by his dying words: "We are beggars, it's true."

DIETRICH BONHOEFFER TO MARIA VON WEDEMEYER,
FROM TEGEL PRISON, 1943

Hoc est Christum cognoscere, beneficia eius cognoscere. *(To know Christ is to know his benefits.)*

PHILIPP MELANCHTHON, *LOCI COMMUNES*, 1521

CHAPTER 2

IN CHRIST:
LIFE FROM THE CROSS

For we do not have a high priest who is unable to sympathize with our weaknesses.

HEBREWS 4:15

There is a certain inclination in human nature to keep off from all problems that might make us feel uncomfortable in our own situation.

DIETRICH BONHOEFFER, LONDON, 1934

Jesus calls men, not to a new religion, but to life.

**DIETRICH BONHOEFFER,
FROM TEGEL PRISON, 1944**

As Hitler came to power and the Nazi Party gained momentum, pressure increased on the German church to acquiesce. A young Dietrich Bonhoeffer, wise well beyond his years, could see the problems acutely. Bonhoeffer championed the cause to stand against the Nazi infiltration in the church. He also championed the cause to stand against the Nazi Party's eugenic crusade. The weak, the mentally and physically challenged, were called "useless eaters." Medical personnel and directors of clinics were ordered to turn over the names of patients. Lists were drawn up. The Nazis mandated the sterilization of these "useless eaters," many of whom simply disappeared. Nothing, or no one, would stand in the way of the "Programme": the cleansing of the German people, the making of the master race. The ascendency of the Aryan race, this was Hitler's dream.

This was not 1940. All of this was already happening in 1933. The outside world, meaning essentially every nation besides Germany, would not be fully awakened to the problem for years to come.[1] Hitler's program of eugenics would march on past the useless eaters, setting its sights on the Jews. By then the world would realize what was happening. But Bonhoeffer, and a tight circle of colleagues, knew all too well where things were headed back in 1933. A churchman by trade, Bonhoeffer looked to the church to take a stand, to lead the people to the truth and justice. But the national church in Germany balked. And then it caved. This would lead to the forming of a reform group within the church, a group of committed and genuine Christians. To Erwin Sutz, a pastor of the Reformed Swiss Church whom Bonhoeffer had met at Union Seminary in New York, Bonhoeffer wrote, "I have been completely absorbed with what is going on in the church. . . . There is no doubt in my mind that the victory will go the German Christians."[2]

We need to understand the context here. In 1931, The German Christians (*Deutsche Christen*) were formed by Ludwig Müller, a longtime Nazi sympathizer. Hitler, having brought the Nazi Party to power in 1933, appointed Müller as his personal confidant in all matters pertaining to the national church, the German Lutheran Church. In September 1933, after the months of bitter struggle that consumed Bonhoeffer, Müller was appointed bishop of the *Reichskirche* (as the church had now come to be called)—and, of all things, it took place at Luther's former cathedral in Wittenberg. Müller sought out Hitler's favor far more than Hitler sought out Müller's. Undeterred, Müller consistently and assiduously put the *Reichskirche* at the service of the Nazis and, later, at that of the Gestapo. In 1945, with Nazi hopes and ideals reduced to rubble, Müller committed suicide.

Though more of a patsy than a capable administrator, Müller did contribute something of significance by bringing the "Aryan Paragraph" (or the "Aryan Clause") into the church, forbidding Jews membership and defrock-

---

[1] Consider Winston Churchill's difficulties in convincing Great Britain's Parliament that Germany was a threat even as late as 1939. Or recall that Charles Lindbergh could only speak of how impressed he was with the German *Luftwaffe* right on up to the eve of the war.

[2] Bonhoeffer to Erwin Sutz, July 17, 1933, *DBWE* 12:140. See also Eberhard Bethge, *Dietrich Bonhoeffer: A Biography*, enl. ed. (Minneapolis: Fortress, 2000), 293–323.

ing Jewish clergy. Müller also stood behind the propaganda campaign that claimed Jesus was not Jewish, but Aryan. In fact, Jesus in the *Reichskirche* and in Nazism was *the* Aryan, the *Übermensch*, the Superman.[3]

Bonhoeffer, though only twenty-seven at the time, took his place among the leaders of the resistance in the church to these horrid moves that would come to have unspeakable consequences during the war. So there came a split within the German church, though to call it a split overestimates Bonhoeffer's dissenting party. *Splinter* fits better, as the vast majority stood by the Nazis. Bonhoeffer, and those of a like mind who formed this splinter group, called it the Confessing Church. These ministers and their parishes would swear allegiance to Christ—who was not Aryan—and not surrender the church to be captive to the political ideology of the Nazi Party.

Like John the Baptist, ministers of the Confessing Church would be the outsiders, raising their prophetic voice to the religious and political establishment. Frustrated by the *Kirchenkampf* (the German Church Struggle, as it was called), and even frustrated by fellow dissenters in the Confessing Church, Bonhoeffer left Germany for some time to live in London.[4] There he would pastor two German Lutheran congregations. While there, he also worked tirelessly to alert the world to what was happening. And especially at this time, he was concerned more with alerting the ecclesiastical world than the political world of the reality of life in Germany. Bonhoeffer may have been living in London, but his heart was turned to Germany.

Übermensch

From 1933 through 1936 the Nazis launched a full-scale public relations war under the watchful eye of Joseph Goebbels, Reich minister of propaganda. The crown jewel of Goebbel's efforts in these early years at his post would be the 1936 Berlin Olympics. As the eyes of the world turned to Germany, Goebbels made sure they would see a pristine, God-fearing country. A lovely church was built right by the Olympic Village.[5]

Bonhoeffer, meanwhile, the outsider prophet, proclaimed the truth.

---

[3] See Bethge, *Dietrich Bonhoeffer*, 304–23; and Susannah Heschel, *The Aryan Jesus: Christian Theologians and the Bible in Nazi Germany* (Princeton, NJ: Princeton University Press, 2012).

[4] Bethge notes how "greatly his views differed from those of his fellow fighters. In nearly all of his suggestions he stood alone." *Dietrich Bonhoeffer*, 325. Much of that difference concerned how theologically driven the Confessing Church would be and what kind of theology that church would espouse, matters picked up in chaps. 4 and 6 below.

[5] For a discussion of this, as well as for the upstaging of Hitler at his own Olympics by African American track star Jesse Owens, see Jeremy Schaap, *Triumph: The Untold Story of Jesse Owens and Hitler's Olympics* (New York: Houghton Mifflin, 2007).

And he preached. His sermons from his "London sojourn," lasting from October 1933 until April 1934, reveal one of the most formative periods in Bonhoeffer's life. He would return to London for short stays throughout 1934 and 1935. The part of the Bonhoeffer story that captivates us is the imprisonment and the final events leading up to his martyrdom. But that prison experience and the richness of his writing during it did not come from a vacuum. Long before his imprisonment Bonhoeffer had embraced certain ideas that had fortified him, given him the courage to stand, deepened his soul, and enabled him to write the kinds of things he wrote.

As an academic, Bonhoeffer had always been intrigued by and committed to ideas. Students and colleagues testify repeatedly to his dogged pursuit of an idea. Many years later, while sitting in Tegel Prison, Bonhoeffer would scratch out a few loose thoughts. Among them he penned, "Something new can always happen in conversation."[6] It was conversations that dominated his relationship with his students. Conversations would start in the late evening and finish off in the early morning hours, as all dimensions of problems would be analyzed like some biologist's dissecting a specimen. Students talked about his lecture style and his courses, but what they remembered the most were the times on the beach or the long walks in the woods—the times when the conversation was all about ideas, or rather a singular idea. Once Bonhoeffer got hold of an idea, he wouldn't let go.

But that's not the kind of embracing of an idea that forged Bonhoeffer's mettle for the unthinkable experiences of the 1940s. Something far surpassing mental apprehension was needed, an idea penetrating Bonhoeffer's very heart and then permeating his entire being. Here is that idea: God's strength is made perfect in our weakness. Bonhoeffer of course first learned this from Paul (2 Cor. 12:9), whose embrace of this idea, like Bonhoeffer's, went far deeper than mental apprehension.

Sometime in 1934, Bonhoeffer preached on 2 Corinthians 12:9 in London.[7] There is no doubt that this idea of divine power made perfect through human weakness had captivated him. There are many dimensions to this idea of God's strength set against our weakness. In our perplexity and confusion, even befuddlement, God's wisdom is displayed. In our frailty and finitude, God's infinity is displayed. But all that cuts across the grain of our natural instincts. Human beings are fueled by the sup-

[6] Bonhoeffer, "Notes," July 1944, LPP, 343.
[7] He likely preached the sermon in late July 1934 during one of his shorter returns to London after his seven-month pastorate, DBWE 13:402n14.

posed limitless possibility of human potential. Like the Olympic motto, "*Citius, Altius, Fortius,*" we strive to be faster, higher, stronger. We don't see ourselves as weak.

It was a German philosopher, Friedrich Nietzsche, who introduced the idea of the *Übermensch*, the Superman, or even more accurately, the *Übermenschen*, the Super Men or the Master Race.[8] Nietzsche despised weakness and frailty. He despised religion, too, especially the religion of the German national Lutheran Church. And he despised Christ. In Nietzsche's world, there is no room for suffering, no room for weakness. Nietzsche would not have applauded the attempts by Müller and the zealous Nazis to make Christ an Aryan. He was more than happy to leave Christ out of the Aryan race altogether.

Now, consider Paul's take on being human, or more importantly, on being a Christian. In a rather autobiographical and self-reflective moment, Paul says, "On my own behalf I will not boast, except of my weaknesses" (2 Cor. 12:5). Nietzsche would not have wanted Paul on his team either.

Pauline Spirituality

Second Corinthians 12:1–10 reveals the things that characterize God and the things that characterize us. In the divine column of the ledger we see strength and power. In the human column we see weakness. In Paul's case the weakness consisted of the ever-mysterious "thorn in the flesh" (12:7), as well as his résumé of, in his own words, "insults, hardships, persecutions, and calamities" (12:10)—not the kinds of things people sign up for.

The idea of God's strength perfected in our weakness, as we've seen, was not something Paul knew merely on an intellectual plane. It was his autobiography, a summary of who he was and what he had gone through. And as he lived his life, he stumbled upon a significant, if not overriding, aspect of this idea: God's grace meets us in and precisely because of our weakness. God said it directly to Paul: "My grace is sufficient for you, for my power is made perfect in weakness" (2 Cor. 12:9). More than a mere piece of autobiographical reflection, this text provides a great deal of insight into Paul's teaching on the Christian life. We should not be surprised, consequently, to find Bonhoeffer looking to this text as he constructs his view of the Christian life.

---

[8] Friedrich Nietzsche, *Thus Spoke Zarathustra*, trans. R. J. Hollingdale (New York: Penguin, 1961), originally published 1883–1885.

On Human Weakness

So why all this emphasis on human weakness? Because human weakness paves the way for God's grace. Human weakness leaves us unable—dependent on something beyond and outside us. Theologians use the word *alien* here, stressing that this something does not come from within, from the *will to power*, as Nietzsche so wrongly put it.

But here's the beauty of this idea. Paul puts a most surprising twist to all of this. For at one point in 1 Corinthians and at one point in 2 Corinthians he refers to *God* as weak. Long before Nietzsche, admired by Hitler as he was, put forth the idea of power, the Romans and the Greeks were obsessed with power. Weakness was not rewarded. On the contrary, power was celebrated. It was the Greeks, after all, who gave us the Olympics. And it was the Romans who built their monuments to their own glory all over the Mediterranean world, the world Paul inhabited.

Along with the obsession with power and strength came the obsession with wisdom, what the New Testament calls worldly or human wisdom. The wisdom the Greeks and Romans applauded was not the reliance on revelation—something outside the human mind, something alien—but rather that which came from within the human mind. Paul refers to this as mere sophistry (1 Cor. 1:20). Human rationality and wisdom, human power and human strength, these were the idols of the first-century culture into which Christ was born and Christianity had its incubation.[9]

Speaking directly to this Greco-Roman culture which celebrated power and wisdom, physical and intellectual heft, Paul writes of the foolishness and the weakness of God (1 Cor. 1:25). Paul later explains a bit more what he means by the weakness of God when, in 2 Corinthians, he speaks of an exact moment in history when this weakness of God occurred. It happened on the cross. So Paul tells us that Christ "was crucified in weakness" (2 Cor. 13:4).

If you're looking for the line of demarcation between what the Greco-Roman worldview had to offer and what Christianity has to offer, this is it. Either hope and redemption reside within human beings so we become the object of our own faith, or hope and redemption reside outside us, alien to us, so we look beyond ourselves to the object of our faith. Only when we come to the end of ourselves do we see our true need. That is the Christian view.

---

[9] Consider John Dickson's thesis that humility was not recognized or touted as a virtue until Jesus Christ and early Christianity, in *Humilitas: A Lost Key to Life, Love, and Leadership* (Grand Rapids: Zondervan, 2011).

And this is patently the line of demarcation between Bonhoeffer's Confessing Church and Müller's *Reichskirche*. Hitler was ultimately and pitifully the object of his own quest for redemption. And his program failed spectacularly.

This is an essential backdrop for understanding Bonhoeffer's view of Christ and the cross. Just as Paul's views of Christ, salvation, and the Christian life were diametrically opposed to the values and presuppositions of the Greco-Roman world, so too Bonhoeffer's views ran completely counter to the ideology of the Nazis. The Nazi worldview praised human strength and human achievement. The cross is truly foolish to such a worldview. But it would be a mistake to limit that faulty view to the Nazis in the twentieth century. In fact, modernism—that worldview which knows no geopolitical boundaries—very much shares this unfettered belief in human wisdom, human power, and human potential. To trumpet, "I will only boast in my weakness," as Paul did and as Bonhoeffer echoed, is to sound a dissonant note to a modernist. Bonhoeffer puts it succinctly: "It is true that encounter with Jesus meant the reversal of all human values."[10] In his unfinished *Ethics*, Bonhoeffer would also write accordingly, "The figure of the judged and crucified one remains alien, and at best pitiable, to a world where success is the measure and justification of all things."[11]

We could summarize all of this background to Bonhoeffer's christology in one sentence, albeit a complex one: The cross was a stumbling block to the Romans; the cross was a stumbling block to the Nazis; the cross was a stumbling block to moderns; and—unless we are humbled and brought low beneath the cross to see its power and beauty—the cross can be a stumbling block to us.

The lesson here is not simply to wag our fingers in disgust at a Nietzsche or a Hitler, but to do a little soul-searching ourselves. Do I think of myself as weak and unable and frail? Or do I think of myself as strong, capable, and able to pull it off? We will not see Christ aright—and, consequently, we will not live the Christian life aright—until we get this question right.

Via Wittenberg

Bonhoeffer did not by himself discover Paul's idea of weakness as the starting point for spirituality and living the Christian life. He had a mediator,

---

[10] Bonhoeffer to Eberhard Bethge, June 30, 1944, *LPP*, 341.
[11] *DBWE* 6:88.

a mentor—none other than the original German Lutheran academic and pastor, Martin Luther himself. For Luther, like Paul before him and Bonhoeffer after, this idea of strength through weakness went much deeper than intellectual approbation. It became warp and woof of their very lives and identities.

Luther had a profound sense of human weakness precisely because he tried so hard. He once quipped, "If ever a monk got to heaven by monkery, I was the monk."[12] To say he was dedicated and committed, to say that he strove for excellence with every fiber of his being, is like saying a lot of water goes over Niagara Falls. But for all that striving, Luther never got any closer to God. It was like he was on a treadmill, and no matter how fast he ran he never got anywhere. In fact, it was worse: the faster he ran, the greater the distance between him and God. As Luther strove toward God, God seemed to move farther and farther beyond his reach.

In this regard Luther was a true child of his age—obsessed with "a theology of glory," as he summarized it. Glory is usually a good thing, but Luther was using it here as shorthand for human achievement, strength, and power. When he criticized the medieval Roman Catholic Church for proclaiming a theology of glory, he was accusing them of trusting in their own might, of relying on their own power. Hence the striving, the dedication, and all the monkery he himself was a part of.

To cut across this theology of glory, Luther proposed a "theology of the cross." It is at the cross that we meet God, and the God we meet at the cross is a God of weakness. This is a God who suffers. And this confounds all human wisdom.[13]

We could easily expand this notion of a God of weakness. From the moment of the incarnation, we see the display of weakness. In fact, we see it even from the moment of the announcement to the Virgin Mary. Bonhoeffer, in one of his London sermons of 1934, makes the case:

> It begins with Mary herself, the carpenter's wife: as we would say, a poor
> working man's wife, unknown, not highly regarded by others; yet now,
> just as she is, unremarkable and lowly in the eyes of others, regarded by

[12] Martin Luther, cited in Bard Thompson, *Humanists and Reformers: A History of the Renaissance and Reformation* (Grand Rapids: Eerdmans, 1996), 388.

[13] For more on Luther's theology of the cross, see Martin Luther, "The Heidelberg Disputation"; Stephen J. Nichols, *Martin Luther: A Guided Tour of His Life and Thought* (Phillipsburg, NJ: P&R, 2002), 69–85; and Gerhard O. Forde, *On Being a Theologian of the Cross: Reflections on Luther's Heidelberg Disputation* (Grand Rapids: Eerdmans, 1997).

God and chosen to be the mother of the Savior of the world. She was not chosen because of any human merit, not even for being, as she undoubtedly was, deeply devout, nor even for her humility or any other virtue, but entirely and uniquely because it is God's gracious will to love, to choose, to make great what is lowly, unremarkable, considered to be of little value.[14]

A few moments later in the sermon Bonhoeffer adds, "God draws near to the lowly, loving the lost, the unnoticed, the unremarkable, the excluded, the powerless, and the broken."[15] And then we come to the unremarkable, lowly manger. Bonhoeffer offers up two palpable images of the weakness and powerlessness of God: the manger and the cross.

Christ came as a powerless, dependent infant. And though on the cross, the hymn writer reminds us, he could have called ten thousand angels, his full limitations and weakness came to the fore as he suffered and died. In Christ we see the weakness of God.

In Christ

At this point we need to acknowledge that something more profound lies beneath both weakness and power. Behind our weakness lies sin, and behind divine power lies holiness. The true problem consists not of our weakness. Weakness is a symptom, merely pointing to our true problem: sinfulness. And the great gulf between us and God is not merely measured by finite weakness compared to infinite strength. The great gulf consists in our utter sinfulness compared to God's incomparable holiness.

Weakness and strength catch our attention because they stick out above the surface like the proverbial tip of the iceberg. If you could ask survivors of the Titanic, they would tell you that what matters is what lies beneath the surface. We can dodge what we see and we can compensate for appearances. But what defense have we for what lies beneath the surface? The issue there is that God is holy, and we are sinful. These are the two fundamental propositions to life. It's really that simple and, at the same time, that profound. No dodging, no compensating. Nothing within us can overcome this problem.

In his classic book *The Holiness of God*, R. C. Sproul makes this link

---

[14] Bonhoeffer, sermon on Luke 1:46–55, *DBWE* 13:343.
[15] Ibid., 344.

from weakness to sinfulness and from strength to holiness when it comes to the thought of Martin Luther.[16] This dilemma was precisely why Luther blurted out, "I hate God." He came to realize the full force of these two propositions—our sinfulness and God's holiness—and it sent him reeling. Only a third proposition could produce the elusive peace he so desperately sought during his quest to come to terms with God in the monastery.

This third proposition that Luther needed and eventually found was actually a person: Christ, the God-man, the only Mediator between a holy God and sinful humanity. Theologians refer to this as a two-nature christology or the hypostatic union. This means that Christ is two natures, fully human and fully divine, in one person. The Greek word for person, used in the Chalcedonian Creed (AD 451) is *hypostasis*, from which comes the theological expression *hypostatic union*. The early church was plagued by various heresies denying the humanity of Christ and the deity of Christ, followed by heresies related to how the two natures came together in one person.

In his lectures on all this, Bonhoeffer concludes, "The Chalcedonian formula [or Creed] is an objective, living assertion about Christ that goes beyond all conceptual forms. Everything is encompassed in its very clear yet paradoxical agility."[17] This last expression, "paradoxical agility," refers to the presence of mystery in the creed, reflective of the mystery we encounter in the person of Christ. To say full humanity and full deity join together in one person is mystery indeed, one that Bonhoeffer deeply appreciated.

For Bonhoeffer, Christ as the God-man is essential to understanding all of Christ's work, but especially his work of humiliation that culminates with his crucifixion. Bonhoeffer observes, "The God-man who is humiliated is the stumbling block to the pious human being and to the human being, period."[18] It's as if Bonhoeffer's lectures up to this point have been merely a revving up to deliver this line. Christ as the God-man is the stumbling block because this accentuates the absolute holiness of God and the utter sinfulness of humanity and the great, gaping gulf between the two. So we must have Christ as the God-man; we must have this third proposition—this person. There is no hope without him.

The work of Christ immediately brings to mind one of Luther's favorite words, *justification*. Bonhoeffer had much to say about this word as well.

---

[16] R. C. Sproul cleverly titled the chapter "The Insanity of Luther." See Sproul, *The Holiness of God*, 25th anniversary ed. (Lake Mary, FL: Ligonier, 2010), 91–116.
[17] Bonhoeffer, "Lectures on Christology," *DBWE* 12:343.
[18] Ibid., 358.

In his lectures on the history of twentieth-century systematic theology, preserved for us in the form of student notes, Bonhoeffer addresses Christ, justification, God, Scripture, and ethics—all themes dear to his heart and, sadly, occasions for many of his fellow-German theologians to go astray. Of justification, Bonhoeffer begins by reminding us of the way the cross of Christ says no to our effort: "It comes through the cross, the radical No of God, the word telling the person you don't have any possibility of reaching God."[19] There's nothing we can do to reach God, so God does it for us, through Christ. This leads Bonhoeffer to conclude, "Thus human beings receive their righteousness from God alone." Bonhoeffer continues: "This is the reason for the cross. Christology is by nature bound up with the doctrine of justification."[20]

We need, as Bonhoeffer cites the Latin, *iustitia aliena*, an "alien righteousness," or a righteousness that is outside of and apart from us. This is the righteousness that comes to us from God through Christ's work on the cross, by faith. In fact, Bonhoeffer calls faith "the most profound human passivity." Justification is all God's work. Bonhoeffer even speaks of the Spirit's work: "The Holy Spirit allows human beings to believe and to hear that the righteousness of humankind lies entirely in Christ."[21]

Sola Gratia

These three propositions—the holiness of God, the sinfulness of humanity, and the person and work of Christ—form the essence of the gospel. They also form the backbone of spirituality, since they leave room for only one thing, *grace*. Grace comes to us not because of our merits or our accomplishments or our potential. Grace comes to us in spite of all these things. Some say that grace is unconditional; it would be more accurate to say that it is contra-conditional. Grace brings us to Christ, keeps us in Christ, and causes us to grow in Christ. Hence, Christ as the God-man is the stumbling block. We are so sure, *self*-assured, that we can achieve God's approval. But that self-assurance is actually self-deception. The cross shouts a resounding *no!*

These three propositions, and the notion of grace they all underscore, are the theological props not only holding up salvation, but also holding up

---

[19] Bonhoeffer, "The History of Twentieth-Century Systematic Theology, 1931–1932," *DBWE* 11:236. See the editors' note on the history of this text, 177.
[20] Ibid., 237–38.
[21] Ibid., 239.

the Christian life and discipleship. We err when we see these as only having to do with our justification. When we leave these three propositions, and especially grace, at the door of initial salvation and try to walk on without them, we are doomed to a Christian life marked by frustration.

"It's very hard," Luther once wrote, "for a man to believe that God is gracious to him. The human heart can't grasp this."[22] We can't grasp grace because our natural instincts think more in terms of merits and demerits. And since we can't grasp grace, it grasps us. Grace grasps us at salvation and at every waking moment of our lives thereafter.

Theologians like to speak of efficacious grace or soteric grace—grace that saves. It is efficacious because it accomplishes God's purposes. Those purposes may be summed up in terms of how God calls a people unto himself (salvation or the moment of conversion) and conforms that people to the image of his Son, the perfect reflection of glory and holiness (sanctification or the process of living of the Christian life).

To be sure, there are differences between coming to Christ at salvation and growing in Christ in sanctification. As Luther put it in "A Mighty Fortress Is Our God," once we are in Christ, "the Spirit and the gifts are ours." Paul speaks of our being raised in newness of life after we have come to Christ (Rom. 6:1–4). Nevertheless, these three propositions remain true for us from the day of our coming to Christ until we reach the end of our earthly lives: God is holy, we are sinful, and Christ is our only hope. And that hope comes not only through Christ's resurrection, but also through Christ's death on the cross.

Christ's resurrection and his resurrection power are the means for our sanctification. As Easter approached in 1944 and Bonhoeffer sat in his prison cell in Tegel, he wrote to his student and eventual biographer Eberhard Bethge of how Christ's resurrection conquered death and that only from the resurrection of Christ, "a new and purifying wind can blow through our present world." Then he expressed his wish for even a mere few "to live in the light of the resurrection."[23] In his lectures on christology, he castigates those who would deny the historicity of the resurrection, and he makes a clear and definitive statement of the necessity of the empty tomb. "Between the humiliation and exaltation of Christ," Bonhoeffer writes of the cross and ascension, "lies the historical fact of the empty grave. . . . If it

[22] Martin Luther, "Table Talk, No. 137," in Luther's Works, vol. 54, Table Talk, ed. and trans. Theodore G. Tappert (Philadelphia: Fortress, 1967), 19.
[23] Bonhoeffer to Eberhard Bethge, March 27, 1944, LPP, 240.

is not empty, then Christ is not resurrected. It seems as though our 'resurrection faith' is bound up with the story of the empty grave. If the grave were not empty, we would not have our faith."[24] Our faith stands on the historicity of the resurrection.

Paul reminds us that to know Christ is *both* to know the power of Christ's resurrection and to share in Christ's sufferings (Phil. 3:10). Bonhoeffer follows suit, reminding us to focus also on the cross and the weakness of Christ as an additional, crucial means for our growth in knowing Christ and conforming to his image. "We are the church beneath the cross," Bonhoeffer would say.[25] After we have first come to the cross, we must return there again and again. In Christ's suffering and weakness God meets us in our suffering and weakness.

Bonhoeffer at Bethel

Bonhoeffer scholar Bernd Wannenwetsch draws attention to Bonhoeffer's 1933 visit to the city of Bethel, Germany. He contrasts Bonhoeffer's time at Bethel, and what he learned there, with his experience at the city of Buchenwald, and what Hitler attempted to do there. "The time here in Bethel," Bonhoeffer wrote to his grandmother Julie on August 20, 1933, "has left a deep impression on me."[26] That deep impression would have far-reaching consequence for the rest of his theology, his view of sanctification, and even his very life.

With no small level of enthusiasm, Bonhoeffer describes in his letter the participants at the church service at Bethel: "I have just come back from the worship service. It is an extraordinary sight, the whole church filled with crowds of epileptics and other ill persons, interspersed with the deacons and deaconesses who are there to help in case one of them falls."[27] He then adds, "There are elderly tramps who come in off the country roads, the

---

[24] Bonhoeffer, "Lectures on Christology," *DBWE* 12:359–60; cf. 1 Cor. 15:1–28, especially vv. 18–20. In the wake of German theologians after Bonhoeffer, Wolfhart Pannenberg stands out as one who continued this stress on the historicity of the resurrection. The empty tomb is for Pannenberg the linchpin to the deity of Christ and christology. Pannenberg even sees the empty tomb as the starting point for epistemology—the starting point for everything we know and how we know what we know. See Wolfhart Pannenberg, *Systematic Theology*, vol. 2, trans. Geoffrey W. Bromiley (Grand Rapids: Eerdmans, 1994), 343–62. Pannenberg, though, in the end stops shy of a full subscription to the Chalcedonian Creed. Bonhoeffer, on the other hand, appreciates the mystery of the Chalcedonian Creed, which reflects the mystery in the union of the full humanity and divinity in Christ, the two natures in one person (*DBWE* 12:342–43).
[25] Bonhoeffer, devotional, Berlin Technical University, 1932, in *Dietrich Bonhoeffer: Meditations on the Cross*, ed. Manfred Weber, trans. Douglas W. Stott (Louisville: Westminster John Knox, 1996), 8.
[26] *DBWE* 12:157.
[27] *DBWE* 12:157–58.

theological students, the children from the lab school, doctors and pastors with their families." He quickly points out, "But the sick people dominate the picture."[28]

This eclectic and diverse mix of worshipers comes as a result of the place, Bethel. At Bethel, just outside the city of Bielefeld, a community was established as a hospital and care facility for the disabled. Bethel also housed a seminary. Bonhoeffer went to Bethel between stays in London. He would spend the month of July in London, preaching a few times and scouting out the church situation there. Then he spent August at Bethel, intending some time for relaxation after a busy cycle of lectures at Berlin and after the frustrations of the ecclesiastical battles. He would return to London for his extended stay and pastorate from October 1933 until the late spring weeks of 1934.

Bonhoeffer had hoped to relax in Bethel, but he didn't. Or, rather, he couldn't. In collaboration with Hermann Sasse, who had just moved from his pastoral work in Berlin to an academic post at the University of Erlangen near Nuremberg, Bonhoeffer worked feverishly on a confession of faith for the splinter group from the German church. While the Bethel Confession would be eclipsed by the Barmen Declaration (1934), the document shows significant differences between the splinter group and the main body of the German Lutheran Church. The acquiescence to Hitler and the Nazi Party was "the presenting problem," as counselors might say; the real issue, however, concerned Scripture. Does the church take Scripture and all of its demands seriously? That, to Bonhoeffer, was the bottom-line question of the controversies of the hour. And as he saw things, his church did not submit to Scripture.

In fact, though we'll explore this further in chapter 4, this is one of the most fundamental questions for us to ask as disciples: Do we take Scripture and all of its demands seriously? We will have a warped view of the Christian life if we see Scripture as something to be negotiated rather than obeyed.

Christ at Bethel

In light of Bonhoeffer's ability to see to the heart of the matter, through the Bethel Confession Bonhoeffer addresses far deeper issues than simply the church-state relationship between the Reich and the Reich Church. As

---

[28] DBWE 12:158.

Bethge puts it so well, "Bonhoeffer, though thoroughly shaped by a liberal tradition, was growing antiliberal."[29] Two theological issues in particular were responsible for this widening gulf between Bonhoeffer's conservative theologizing and his liberal education and context: Scripture and christology.

In his Berlin lectures on christology, published as *Christ the Center* from the notes of his students, Bonhoeffer makes it clear that "Christ as idea" or "Christ as myth" simply won't do. Bonhoeffer declares, "It is not so, as Wilhelm Herrmann says, that our conscience in its distress encounters Jesus in our inner life, and that through this encounter we become convinced that Jesus existed in history."[30] Jesus is in reality, in space-and-time history, not an abiding idea within. "The church must reject every form of docetism," Bonhoeffer would go on to lecture. "Along with it we must refuse every form of Greek idealistic thinking to the extent that it works with the distinction between idea and appearance." Docetism was a generic name applied to a variety of heresies in the era of the New Testament and in the early centuries of the church. The Greek word *dokeō* means "appear." This heresy taught that Jesus only appeared to be human; he only appeared to be in flesh and blood. The apostle John himself refutes this false teaching (1 John 4:1–4).

Bonhoeffer explains why this false thinking about Christ is so out of bounds: "For with this distinction, such idealism abolishes the first premise of all theology, that God, out of mercy freely given, truly became a human being."[31] "Nothing human," Bonhoeffer will later add, "is foreign to him."[32] Bonhoeffer later draws upon the humiliation of Christ—his becoming human and suffering and eventually meeting judgment on the cross— as a hallmark of the true church. This is what the church must confess (orthodoxy) and this confession must impact how we in the church live ("orthopraxy").

Only a Christ who was truly human, who *really* came in the flesh, and who simultaneously was very God of very God would be sufficient for the church's stance in any time and place, but especially in the tumultuous time and precarious place of the rising Reich and *Reichskirche* in 1933 Germany. Only such a Christ can eclipse human kingdoms and demand our

---

[29] Bethge, *Dietrich Bonhoeffer*, 289.
[30] Bonhoeffer, "Lectures on Christology," *DBWE* 12:330. His lecture series, again as recorded by students, is also published as *Christ the Center* (New York: HarperOne, 1978).
[31] *DBWE* 12:338.
[32] *DBWE* 12:353.

allegiance above all else, as the Barmen Declaration will so definitively exclaim. To put the whole matter succinctly, christology is the key for understanding Bonhoeffer's theology and also his view of the Christian life.

But in the midst of his ecclesiastical work and theologizing, Bonhoeffer couldn't help but be moved, "deeply impressed," by what he saw at Bethel. On the one side stood Hitler and his eugenic plan for German superiority, already revealed and initiated at that time. On the other side stood Bethel, haven for the sick, the infirm, and the weak. That it was called Bethel, "house of God," was not at all lost on Bonhoeffer. He saw in Bethel far more than the church as a place of variety and diversity. He saw in Bethel true humanity. To his grandmother he writes, "Their situation of being truly defenseless perhaps gives these people a much clearer insight into certain realities of human existence, the fact that we are indeed basically defenseless, than can be possible for healthy persons."[33]

Bethel provided Bonhoeffer with insight into the nature of humanity and even into the nature of the church. It also provided him with insight into the nature of Christ. In the early summer of 1933, before he went to Bethel, Bonhoeffer gave his aforementioned christology lectures at Berlin. Near the very end of the lectures, when discussing the humiliation and exaltation of Christ, he observes, "The humiliation of Christ is not a principle for the church to follow but rather a fact."[34]

Theologians use the language of the humiliation and exaltation of Christ in reference to Paul's teaching in Philippians 2 on the person and work of Christ. Philippians 2 is among Scripture's fuller statements on two-nature christology, on Christ as the God-man. What we learn in this chapter concerning Christ's humanity thrusts us right back to this idea of Christ's weakness and suffering. In the larger context of Philippians 2 we also see how crucial learning this lesson is for living the Christian life. Humility becomes for Paul the necessary ingredient for church life. And that humility comes to life in Christians who imitate Christ, the one whose humility exceeds all bounds, even the bounds of death on the cross. Bonhoeffer would also bring the full weight of Christ's example of humiliation—of suffering and weakness and of frailty and limitation—to bear upon being a disciple when he got back to London and took to the pulpits of the United Congregation of Sydenham and St. Paul's Reformed Church in East London.

---

[33] *DBWE* 13:158.
[34] *DBWE* 13:360.

Sermons in London

Before we consider Bonhoeffer's London sermons, and one sermon in particular, it is helpful to see one more of his Berlin lectures from early summer of 1933, entitled "What Should a Student of Theology Do Today?" To answer his own question Bonhoeffer states,

> The real study of *theologia sacra* [sacred theology] begins when, in the midst of questioning and seeking, human beings encounter the cross; when they recognize the endpoint of all their own passions in the suffering of God at the hands of humankind, and realize that their entire vitality stands under judgment.[35]

Bonhoeffer wouldn't mind extending the application. This is not merely the requisite for academic theology students. It is the requisite for us all. We all start at the cross. All encounters with God begin there. Bonhoeffer's message was the same. He preached or proclaimed the same ideas whether he was in the classroom in Berlin with a room full of future pastors and theologians or he was in the pulpit in London before a largely working class congregation of German immigrants.

One of Bonhoeffer's London sermons in particular brings all of this discussion to a head. The handwritten manuscript of his sermon on 2 Corinthians 12:9 is in English. The congregation at St. Paul's Reformed Church included many who had already assimilated into British culture, forcing Bonhoeffer to preach in his second language. It is a sermon on weakness, and Bonhoeffer rightly opens with a question, "Why is this problem of weakness so all-important?"[36] The first answer is that Christianity has historically been the religion of the weak, a "religion of slaves" as Bonhoeffer calls it.[37] But the real answer is that suffering and weakness are holy because "our God is a suffering God," and "God has suffered on the cross."[38]

In *Ethics*, Bonhoeffer will say similarly that God not merely embraces human beings. In fact, to say as much "is not enough."[39] God does far more than embrace us. In Christ he becomes us.

> God overrules every reproach of untruth, doubt, and uncertainty, raised against God's love by entering as a human being into human life, by tak-

[35] *DBWE* 12:433.
[36] *DBWE* 13:401.
[37] *DBWE* 13:402.
[38] *DBWE* 13:403.
[39] *DBWE* 6:84.

ing on and bearing bodily the nature, essence, guilt, and suffering of human beings. God becomes human out of love for humanity. God does not seek the most perfect human being with whom to be united but takes on human nature as it is. Jesus Christ is not the transfiguration of noble humanity but the Yes of God to real human beings, not the dispassionate yes of a judge but the merciful yes of a compassionate sufferer.[40]

We prefer to avoid such topics as weakness and suffering. Instead, we celebrate power. In fact, going back to his London sermon, Bonhoeffer contrasts this Christian view, stressing as it does weakness, with what he terms the aristocratic view, stressing strength and power. He also sets his targets on the means by which the aristocratic view accomplishes its ends, the means of violence and oppression. "Christianity stands or falls with its revolutionary protest against violence," Bonhoeffer thunders in the sermon, "against arbitrariness and pride of power and with its apologia for the weak."[41] No doubt he has Bethel in mind when he spins off this last sentence. He also has in mind what will come to be represented in Buchenwald and Flossenbürg and the other concentration camps when he solemnly points out, "Christianity has adjusted itself much too easily to the worship of power."[42]

The situation, as Bonhoeffer sees it, calls for nothing other than a Copernican revolution in worldview, or as Bonhoeffer put it himself, "a new order of values in the sight of Christ."[43] Power no longer asserts itself, but submits and defers. So Bonhoeffer insists, "Christian love and help for the weak means humiliation of the strong before the weak, of the healthy before the suffering, of the mighty before the exploited."[44]

Bonhoeffer cast a broader vision here than one solely focused on Germany. He mentions, in the course of the sermon, the exploitation of "a coloured man in a white country," referring to his experiences in a black Harlem church in New York City as 1929 rolled into 1930.[45] He also refers to the experiences of the "untouchable," referring to his long-distance appreciation for Ghandi's work in India and the oppressive caste system there.

[40] DBWE 6:84–85. That Bonhoeffer is here thinking of christology as counter to the Aryan way is clear when in the very next paragraph he contrasts God as the lover of humanity with Hitler, "the tyrannical despiser of humanity."
[41] DBWE 13:402.
[42] DBWE 13:402.
[43] DBWE 13:403.
[44] DBWE 13:403.
[45] DBWE 13:402.

In short, Bonhoeffer was questioning the new values of the twentieth century regarding the estimation of life. Or maybe there's nothing all that new about twentieth-century perspectives after all.

Bonhoeffer saw implications within an orthodox christology for how one lives. By coming to grips with our own sinfulness we cultivate a little humility. By coming to grips with Christ's *humiliation* and his taking on flesh and fully identifying with us, we cultivate a little more humility (Philippians 2). And from this stance of humility comes service to others.

Based on what Bonhoeffer learned of Christ and of his incarnation and cross work, Bonhoeffer proceeded to turn the worldview of his contemporaries upside down. A very close next step after this christology concerns how we as disciples view people, how we treat them, and the lengths to which we are willing to serve them. Our natural inclination tilts far more inward. Christ's humiliation forces us first upward to look to him, then outward to look to others.

No doubt the London congregation sensed something heavily pressing upon Bonhoeffer. It's intriguing to be around someone who is on to something. Such a person has a way of drawing you in. So it was for Bonhoeffer, and so it was for his congregation. And once they were drawn in to an understanding of the depth and length and breadth of what being a disciple means, he led them right back to the cross in his conclusion. The man who goes to the cross finds God's strength manifest in weakness and suffering, and as Bonhoeffer offers, "There he feels God being with him, there he is open for God's strength, that is God's grace, God's love, God's comfort, which passeth all understanding and all human values." He then crescendos, "God glorifies himself in the weak as He glorified himself in the cross. God is mighty where man is nothing."[46]

These experiences from 1933 and 1934 are formative in Bonhoeffer's life. The Berlin lectures on christology, the time at Bethel, the writing of the Bethel Confession, and his London pastorate all shaped him in definitive ways. We'll see in the next chapter how the idea of community—a concept for Bonhoeffer that can only flow from Christ and the cross—also shaped both the actions of his life and his theology. Taken together, these twin ideas of Christ and community, hammered out in the 1930s, are responsible for the heroic moments to come in Bonhoeffer's life of the 1940s.

---

[46] *DBWE* 13:404.

Heroic Christianity

It was during one of those moments in the 1940s that his mind took him back to his earlier travels. He spent the last year of the so-called Roaring Twenties in New York City. His studies at Union Seminary, the ostensible reason for his visit, left him a bit chagrined. He found his most enjoyable moments in the Abyssinian Baptist Church in Harlem, collecting Negro spiritual and early blues seventy-eights and taking a cross-country trip. Everywhere he went he plunged himself into local life, and on his road trip, he saw plenty of it. Some things in America left him nonplussed. Prohibition made no sense. "How frightfully tedious," he wrote in a letter to his twin sister, Sabine.[47] He was equally bored by the theater: "The Theater programs here are usually quite dreadful, so I rarely go." He could even say that Arturo Toscanini helming the New York Philharmonic "hasn't really moved me much."[48] But the road trip west and south to Mexico in the summer of 1930 would be something else altogether.

The trip's impact on Bonhoeffer was made in no small part by his companions, especially Jean Lasserre, who would later pastor Reformed Churches in France. Lasserre's intensity alone caught Bonhoeffer's attention, but the substance of his thought and commitment kept Bonhoeffer listening.

So deep was the impact that decades later, sitting in his jail cell in Tegel Prison, Bonhoeffer would recall conversations with Lasserre, presumably in a pup tent somewhere alongside one of America's highways. It was the kind of conversation had by young men with good starts and bright futures. They talked about what they wanted to do with their lives. Lasserre, Bonhoeffer recalls, "said he would like to be a saint." Still remembering the conversation, Bonhoeffer adds, "At the time I was very impressed, but I disagreed with him, and said, in effect, that I should like to learn to have faith." He further explains the kind of faith he meant:

> I discovered later, and I'm still discovering right up to this moment, that it is only by living completely in this world that one learns to have faith. One must completely abandon any attempt to make something of oneself, whether it be a saint, or a converted sinner, or a churchman (so-called priestly-type!), a righteous one or an unrighteous one, a sick man or a healthy.[49]

---

[47] *DBWE* 10:271.
[48] *DBWE* 10:271.
[49] Bonhoeffer to Eberhard Bethge, July 21, 1944, *LPP*, 369–70.

One could likely add to the list *hero*, a word used so many times in reference to Bonhoeffer and one he would resist with every fiber of his being. The kind of living by faith Bonhoeffer longed to have back in America in the summer of 1930 and in Tegel in the summer of 1944, as well as the summers in between, eschewed the goals we typically set for our lives and the benchmarks we use to estimate our lives. And that kind of faith comes by our union with Christ and staying close to the cross. Actually, at this time, Bonhoeffer was thinking of Christ at Gethsemane. So he writes, "I mean living unreservedly in life's duties, problems, successes and failures, experiences and perplexities. In so doing we throw ourselves completely into the arms of God, taking seriously not our own sufferings, but those of God in the world—watching with Christ in Gethsemane."[50] Bonhoeffer learned to embrace the perplexities, the failures, the suffering, and the times when his weakness was right up on the surface and in plain view.

This isn't the sort of talk one hears orbiting conversations on spirituality and living the Christian life. We tend to prefer the language of victory, of achievement and accomplishment, and of success and overcoming. We prefer a more heroic Christianity. It's likely that a book on weakling Christianity would either be perceived as a joke or be dismissed with a shrug.

Bonhoeffer realized, though, that a theology of the Christian life which flows from the cross offers a different metric than that of heroism and victory. "How can success make us arrogant," he writes, "or failure lead us astray, when we share in God's sufferings through a life of this kind?" So Bonhoeffer can affirm, while in a prison cell as his hopes for release and (far more of concern to him) his hopes for temporal justice ebb away with each bit of news received, "I'm grateful for the past and present, and content with them."[51] To be able to say such words and to live such a contented life comes only in grasping what faith is really all about. And even at that, we need to remember that our faith is a gift.

It is ironic that decades, even an entire generation, later we have made so much of Dietrich Bonhoeffer, his courage, and his heroic efforts. He would have no problem with being an example. In fact, while in prison he sketched out a book, one of many, he would never write. In the concluding chapter he asserts, "[The church] must not underestimate the importance of human example (which has its origins in the humanity of Jesus and is

---

[50] Ibid., 370.
[51] Ibid.

so important in Paul's teaching)."[52] That Bonhoeffer is used as an example would likely embarrass him, but it would not be met with a reprimand; as an exemplar of heroism is another thing altogether. He would issue a rebuke, reminding us that it is only in our weakness that God's strength is displayed. When we say we are nothing, as he concluded his London sermon on 2 Corinthians 12:9, we are finally on the right track to becoming something *in Christ*. Bonhoeffer's example is in this: Christ is magnified in his life, in his sufferings, in his perplexities, and in his joys.

Jesus himself taught that he "must suffer many things" (Luke 9:22). In fact, after his death, he also reminded the two disciples on the road to Emmaus that he must "suffer these things" (Luke 24:26). His suffering meant rejection and it meant crucifixion—the ultimate sacrifice of love in laying down his life for his people. And after his suffering, rejection, and death on the cross, as he told those same two traveling disciples, he "enter[s] into his glory" (Luke 24:26).

Christ follows up his earlier self-reference to suffering in Luke 9:22 with a clarion call to commitment: "If anyone would come after me, let him deny himself and take up his cross and follow me" (Luke 9:23). Any would-be disciple is called upon to face both suffering and rejection, the experience of weakness and oppression. "Outsider status" becomes the hallmark of Jesus and his followers. This verse, which Bonhoeffer mulled over while in London, stands behind and under and all around his classic text *The Cost of Discipleship*. Again, as we have already seen, whenever we look into Bonhoeffer on living the Christian life, we are always bumping into Bonhoeffer's christology.

Discipleship as Living in Christ, in Community, in Love

Bonhoeffer, though, noticed something about the words "in Christ" as he surveyed his current landscape. He noticed their absence. In fact, he noticed a more fundamental absence, the absence of Christ himself. As he put it, "Jesus is disappearing from sight."[53] This comment comes in the context of Bonhoeffer's estimation of the Protestant denominations, such as his own German Lutheran Church. The Jesus that disappeared was the crucified Jesus, the humiliated Jesus, the Jesus who himself taught that he "must suffer many things." In a profound irony, the Lutheran Church—the

---

[52] Bonhoeffer, "Outline for a Book," *LPP*, 383.
[53] Ibid., 381.

church that claimed to be following in Luther's footsteps—was forgetting the theology of the cross.

Bonhoeffer had been thinking this way long before he went to prison. In a 1932 sermon preached in Berlin, even before Hitler's coming to power, Bonhoeffer contrasted invoking God's name instead of Christ's. How safe it is to say, "in the name of God." It is another thing altogether to say, "You have been raised in Christ," from Colossians 3:1, his text for the sermon.[54]

While the church could not see Jesus, let alone have him as Lord over them, Bonhoeffer saw clearly that the church must have Jesus at the center and that the church must have room for the Jesus who suffers. In the outline for the book he never wrote, Bonhoeffer also spoke of Jesus the crucified as the model for us. As the crucified one, Jesus suffered rejection. As the crucified one, Jesus came and acted and lived for others. As the crucified one, Jesus, having lived a sacrificial life of love for others, died a sacrificial death in love for others. This serves as both the basis for and the model of living the Christian life. This is the basis and model for Bonhoeffer's theology of spirituality.

From his christology, which entails a robust and orthodox view of the God-man and of the sacrificial life, atoning death, and triumphant resurrection of Christ, flows all of Bonhoeffer's theology and ethics. In fact, as we've noted, Bonhoeffer scholars have recently taken to identifying the center of all of his thought as "Christo-ecclesiology." What that expression means is not that he simply emphasized christology and ecclesiology, but that his ecclesiology, seen in such books as *Life Together*, flows from and is connected to his christology. This is more than a symbiotic relationship. This is even more than a case of cookies *and* milk or of Romeo *and* Juliet.

But there is one more piece to the picture of Bonhoeffer's theology. That piece is ethics. So, while this may be cumbersome, we can identify the center of Bonhoeffer's thought as "Christo-ecclesiological-ethics." Or we could simply say that according to Bonhoeffer, *life is lived in Christ, in community, in love.*

The kind of grasping and embracing of Christ that Bonhoeffer talks about demands ethics, that we live for others in a sacrificial, loving way. To anticipate some of the themes in the next chapter, Bonhoeffer declares that "the church is the church only when it exists for others."[55] If we start

---

[54] Dietrich Bonhoeffer, "Risen with Christ," in *The Collected Sermons of Dietrich Bonhoeffer*, ed. Isabel Best (Minneapolis: Fortress, 2012), 41–48.
[55] Bonhoeffer, "Outline for a Book," *LPP*, 382.

with the church, we are pushed back to Christ and pushed forward to a life of love for others, a life of action for others. This for Bonhoeffer was both theory and practice. And as for us, we could do no better than to have such a Christo-ecclesiological-ethic. We could do no better than *to live in Christ, in community, in love.*

Conclusion: Christ and the Cost of Discipleship

Those familiar with Bonhoeffer will likely wonder why in a discussion of the foundation of Bonhoeffer's thought on the Christian life his classic book on the subject, *The Cost of Discipleship*, has only been briefly mentioned. Now's the time to rectify that. *The Cost of Discipleship* (the German title is simply *Nachfolge*) was published in 1937, but Bonhoeffer began thinking about the book in 1933 and 1934 during his time in London. Once he returned to Germany, he worked on the book in earnest in 1935, putting the finishing touches on it in 1936. The years of the book's coming to life, in other words, correspond directly with the formative years of the 1930s that have been our subject in this chapter. And while he worked on the book from its inception in 1933 until its publication in 1937, he *lived* the book pretty nearly his entire life. He certainly lived it as the 1930s ebbed into the 1940s and he found himself in prison and on the martyr's gallows.

The book could not be clearer. "Discipleship is commitment to Christ," Bonhoeffer writes.[56] Christ calls, we follow. That much is straightforward, even easy. The doing of it is another story. By chapter 6, Bonhoeffer leads us to the Sermon on the Mount and the difficulties in the simple command to follow Christ. These are heavy demands. But we must not run to chapter 6 and the following chapters of his book without spending time at chapter 4, "Discipleship and the Cross."

Bonhoeffer starts this chapter with Christ's word that he must suffer, be rejected, and die. He uses Mark 8:31–38, which parallels Luke 9. Here Bonhoeffer reminds us of Christ's imperative: we must, like Christ, take up our cross and share in his suffering. Bonhoeffer ticks off what this entails. "The first Christ-suffering that everyone has to experience is the call which summons us away from our attachments to this world. It is the death of the old self in the encounter with Jesus Christ."[57] This death, though, is the beginning of our life, our life *in Christ.* Second, this following of Christ in his

---

[56] DBWE 4:59.
[57] DBWE 4:87.

suffering leads us into our everyday battles with temptation and our daily struggles with sin and Satan. These battles leave scars.

But then Bonhoeffer offers words of comfort. "Christian suffering is not disconcerting," he assures us. "Instead, it is nothing but grace and joy."[58] Christ not only suffered, but bore the suffering on the cross. In his bearing of the suffering, he triumphed over it. Bonhoeffer puts it plainly, "His cross is the triumph over suffering."[59] We are called to such a life. We follow Christ "under the cross."[60]

We might prefer to slip out from under such a call, the burden of bearing the cross. Bonhoeffer points us to Christ, both his example and words, when we feel such temptation. In the garden of Gethsemane, Christ provided the example for us by yielding his will to the Father's. Such submission ultimately brought about peace for Christ and reconciliation with the Father. As for Christ's words, Bonhoeffer takes us to Matthew 11:30. He writes of how people desire to and even can "shake off the burdens laid on them."[61] They can slip out from under the cross. But listen to what Bonhoeffer has to say about such a move: "Doing so does not free them at all from their burdens. Instead, it loads them with a heavier, more unbearable burden. They bear the self-chosen yoke of their own selves."[62] So we should hear again Bonhoeffer's salient point from his lectures on christology: "The God-man who is humiliated is the stumbling block to the pious human being and to the human being, period."[63] In other words: God, preserve us from our piety.

Compared to our self-chosen yokes and pious endeavors and white-knuckled strivings, Christ's burden is easy and light. Christ's burden is welcome indeed. So Bonhoeffer concludes:

> Bearing the cross does not bring misery and despair. Rather, it provides refreshment and peace for our souls; it is our greatest joy. Here we are no longer laden with self-made laws and burdens, but with the yoke of him who knows us and who himself goes with us under the same yoke. Under his yoke we are assured of nearness and communion. It is he himself who disciples find when they take up their cross.[64]

---

[58] *DBWE* 4:89.
[59] *DBWE* 4:90.
[60] *DBWE* 4:90.
[61] *DBWE* 4:91.
[62] *DBWE* 4:91.
[63] Bonhoeffer, "Lectures on Christology," *DBWE* 12:358.
[64] *DBWE* 4:91.

For Bonhoeffer, living the Christian life begins with Christ, with his call to discipleship, with the cross. We live *in Christ*. We live from the cross. Or, as Bonhoeffer would prefer, reminding us that we live in community, "We are the church beneath the cross."[65] It is here—oh the paradox!—where our final joy is found.

---

[65] Bonhoeffer, *Meditations on the Cross*, 8.

CHAPTER 3

IN COMMUNITY: LIFE IN THE CHURCH

Christianity means community through Jesus Christ and in Jesus Christ. No Christian community is more or less than this. . . . We belong to one another only through and in Jesus Christ.

DIETRICH BONHOEFFER, *LIFE TOGETHER*, 1938

The church is the church only when it exists for others.

**DIETRICH BONHOEFFER,
FROM TEGEL PRISON, 1944**

While in prison at Tegel, Dietrich Bonhoeffer wrote a novel. He also wrote a play, a short story, poems, batches of letters, lectures, and sermons for various occasions. These sermons—for weddings and funerals of relatives and former students and friends—were smuggled out of prison and read for him in absentia. Bonhoeffer was, as Eric Metaxas dubbed him in the subtitle to his biography, a "pastor, martyr, prophet, spy." But Bonhoeffer was also a writer. Much of what he wrote was nonfiction, some of which has already taken its rightful place in the history of Christian thought as classic texts, but he also wrote fiction. The volume comprising his fiction in the sixteen-volume set of his collected works is admittedly slim. But the volume is there, and in it is his novel. Bonhoeffer, pastor and theologian, martyr and some-time spy, wrote a novel.

Magazine editor Shirley Abbott once quipped that "all fiction may be autobiography." Such is not far off the mark for Bonhoeffer's novel. The opening scene introduces us to the main character, Frau Karoline Brake, with parasol in hand, walking home from church. She stops at a park bench and recalls a conversation she had with her grandson as they once walked home from church, having heard what she could only call "another miserable sermon."[1] Her grandson, it turns out, had little patience for church and for such sermons. In fact, her whole family felt the same way. One by one, her husband—who also happened to be the mayor—her sons and daughters, and her grandchildren all slipped away. And so she found herself alone on Sundays. Walking alone to church, sitting alone in church, and returning home alone from church—that was Frau Brake.

Eventually she would have given up on church, too. As Bonhoeffer reveals an aspect of his main character, however, "she was not the kind who gave up easily."[2] Frau Karoline Brake was of durable stock, straightforward, one who told it like it is. Church was bad because the sermons were bad, and the sermons were bad because "hot air had taken the place of God's Word."[3] She knew her church had left behind its charge and calling. But she wouldn't give up without a fight.

So, while seated on that park bench and recalling the conversation she had with her grandson, Frau Brake thinks of something she wishes she had said to him at the time. In the conversation he told her, in effect, that he had outgrown church, no longer needing those "miserable sermons." She wishes she had reached down, grasped his hand, looked him straight in the eye, and declared, "You mustn't confuse Christianity with its pathetic representative."[4] She wishes she had said it to him, but she hadn't.

Frau Brake no doubt represents Bonhoeffer's own grandmother, Julie [Tafel] Bonhoeffer. The grandson is Bonhoeffer, who as the novel unfolds will progress beyond his youthful smugness. And the church all too well represents the German church Bonhoeffer was a part of and then broke

---

[1] Bonhoeffer, *Sunday*, unpublished novel, *DBWE* 7:73. Bonhoeffer wrote similar estimations of the sermons he heard from Harry Emerson Fosdick and others during his second visit to America in 1939. Those actual sermons were preached in June and, like this fictional one, in July. See Bonhoeffer, "American Diary," *DBWE* 15:217–45. Of Fosdick's sermon in particular, he remarked, "Simply unbearable," *DBWE* 15:224. We'll return to the American sermons he heard in chap. 6 below.
[2] *DBWE* 7:75.
[3] *DBWE* 7:74.
[4] *DBWE* 7:74.

from. One editor at a German publishing house that was considering the novel called it "meditations on family history."[5] So the saying rings true about fiction being autobiographical.

Bonhoeffer's fiction is not only autobiographical but also theological, which should come as no surprise by now. Only a theologian would choose as the opening scene a walk home from church and a discussion of the sermon. He has Frau Brake dismissing the church as a pathetic representation of the real thing because that's what his decade and a half of *Kirchenkampf* (church struggles) were all about. In many ways, that's what his vocation was all about: calling the church out, calling the church to be the real thing. For Bonhoeffer, that meant preaching the Word and being true to its confession and doctrine. As the novel unfolds, Bonhoeffer adds one more criterion to the list of the genuine church. The church is the real thing when it is not consumed with the assertion of power in culture, but it is driven by service to others. The word *ministry* translates the Greek word *diakonia*, which means service. The church must be about serving others. When a church can lay claim to all three criteria, namely, preaching of the Word, being true to its confession, and focusing on serving, then it's a church worth going to. And then it's a church full of sermons worth listening to.

Bonhoeffer clearly had an agenda in writing his novel. That's not to say, however, one should overlook the literary merit of the novel. Bonhoeffer had a rare combination of gifts in being both a good theologian and a good writer.

From Novels to Dissertations

His novel, which he called *Sunday*, was one of his last writings. It speaks of the same topic and has the same perspective as his first published writing, *Sanctorum Communio* (*The Communion of Saints*).[6] The topic is the nature of the church. And that first book, published in 1930, came out as Bonhoeffer turned twenty-four years old. It was a revision of his dissertation. Interestingly, from the span of his writing from 1927 right on through 1944, and from dissertations and seminar papers right on through to poems and a novel, Bonhoeffer kept circling back to the topic of the church. It was his first love.

Like most doctoral students, Bonhoeffer needed to write in the area of

---

[5] From the introduction, *DBWE* 7:8.
[6] See *DBWE* 1.

his advisor and of the faculty of his program. This put young Dietrich—who started his doctoral work as a nineteen-year-old—in a bit of a bind. One side of the faculty stressed theology and divine revelation; the other side stressed sociology and what is sometimes called historicism. The differences were sharp and defined, the line in the sand made clear.

The difference could be put this way. Is the church and what it believes a product of the divine, from above? Or is the church and what it believes a more horizontal product, one that grows out of human experience and is necessarily culturally conditioned and proscribed? Historicism and the sociological model go with the latter, even placing the Bible itself firmly on the plane of the horizontal. Historicists claim that all matters pertaining to the Bible and theology are necessarily culturally conditioned and created. Religion and Christianity, they say, are nothing more than sociology. The opposing view stresses God's revelation, the Bible, as a top-down product. God revealed his will—certainly to a people in culture, in a time and place—but God is the author. He is the actor, the initiator, the sovereign overseer. In this view Christianity and religion are *theology*, not sociology. The Christian religion is divine in origin, not human.

As a student at Berlin in the 1920s, Bonhoeffer found himself squarely in the middle of the liberal-conservative battle. The conservative side was in the minority. Had he been more calculating, Bonhoeffer would have gone the sociological/historicist route. His mother, Paula, advised that he pursue a topic of church history, that he write on Luther and consequently not get entangled in the fray. There would be time enough later to write on theology, she told him. "Rethink this," she wrote with all the earnestness of a caring mother.[7] But like his character Frau Brake, he had a little fight in him. Bonhoeffer not only chose to write on the church, but also produced a *theological* study of the church. Yet he was nobody's fool, so he entitled his work *Sanctorum Communio: A Theological Study of the Sociology of the Church*. Bonhoeffer completed his seminars, passed his exams, and submitted his dissertation—all by July 1927, and all at the age of twenty-one. He entered the fray and he came out standing.

What is the church? This is the question that dogged him as a young theological student, that became the subject of his dissertation, that would stare him in the face in his early career as minister and theologian, that would drag him into the ring during church struggles through the 1930s

---

[7] Paula Bonhoeffer to Dietrich Bonhoeffer, August 31, 1925, *DBWE* 9:148.

and on into the war years, and that would be the ever-present subject in the pages of his one and only novel. Ecclesiology is at the center of Bonhoeffer's thought.

His ecclesiology, though, is never an independent topic. It always flows from and back to Christ and his christology. Neither is Bonhoeffer content with mere academic work on ecclesiology. For his ecclesiology is never independent of practice or action. Christ always and necessarily stands before and above and over Bonhoeffer's ecclesiology; and ethics, which for him can be summed up in love, always and necessarily pours out from and surrounds his ecclesiology.

| CHRISTOLOGY | → | ECCLESIOLOGY | → | ETHICS/LIFE |
| IN CHRIST | | IN COMMUNITY | | IN LOVE |

What Is the Church?

It's worth exploring Bonhoeffer's answer to the question he takes up in his dissertation, what is the church? He begins his answer by asking, what is a person? since the church as community is made up of persons, and he points out a few things about the Christian notion of person. First, "the human person originates only in relation to the divine."[8] We are created by God. Second, we are social beings. In fact, "the individual belongs essentially and absolutely with the other."[9] Community with God and social community define personhood, Bonhoeffer argues in chapter 2 of his dissertation. But "a rupture has come into the unbroken community."[10] He explains, "A third power, sin, has stepped between human beings and God, as between human beings themselves."[11] Sin sets askew the vertical divine-human relationship and the horizontal human-human relationship. As Bonhoeffer states later in the dissertation, "The fall replaced love with selfishness."[12]

We have stumbled here upon the problem of the human condition, the sense that something is not right with us and not right with the world. Various philosophies, religions, even the state step in at this point to offer solutions to the human condition. Bonhoeffer saw such attempts in his native Germany. But none of those suffice. To set everything right, we need Christ.

---

[8] *DBWE* 1:49.
[9] *DBWE* 1:56.
[10] *DBWE* 1:63.
[11] *DBWE* 1:63.
[12] *DBWE* 1:107.

Christ remakes us. In Christ, we are again reconciled to God and again reconciled to each other. In Christ, we are truly persons. Christ overcomes the human condition. The crucified and risen Christ becomes "God's incarnate love for us—as God's will to renew the covenant, to establish God's rule and thus to create community."[13] It is Christ's action as "vicarious representative" that makes the crucial difference.[14] The community between God and humanity is restored, and "the community of human beings with each other has also become a reality in love once again."[15]

In Bonhoeffer's view, Christ not only has made the church possible; he also has "realized" the church, bringing it into reality and remaining at the center of it. The New Testament metaphors for the church bear this out. We are Christ's bride, Christ is the Head of the body, the chief cornerstone of the building—all of which indicate that the church is "in and through Christ."[16] So we start with Christ. First, the community finds its beginnings, ending, and center in and through *Christ*. Second, the *Holy Spirit*, working through the Word, brings us into this community. Third, *faith*, enabled by God through the Spirit drawing us to him, grants us entry into this community. Finally, *love* is the hallmark of this community. Leaning on Augustine's insight, Bonhoeffer sees the *sanctorum communio* as "the community of loving persons who, touched by God's Spirit, radiate love and grace."[17]

These four—Christ, the Holy Spirit, faith, and love—constitute Bonhoeffer's sense of the church. This sets the church apart from every vain attempt of philosophers or kings or gurus or any other person to establish community. In all of those other paradigms, the divine-human community is missing. The church, the communion of the saints, is the only true community.

Loving Jesus, Not the Church?

The word *community* has played a significant role in our own time. There's a new joke making the rounds. In previous generations, the answer to every Sunday school question was "Jesus." Today, the answer is always "community"! Good ideas, like that of recovering community, can sometimes run away with themselves.

---

[13] *DBWE* 1:154.
[14] *DBWE* 1:155.
[15] *DBWE* 1:157.
[16] *DBWE* 1:157, emphasis added.
[17] *DBWE* 1:175.

Moving from Bonhoeffer's time to ours, there is a tendency to diminish if not dismiss the organized church and to opt instead for this abstract idea of community. At some places along the continuum of the emergent church such a sentiment can be found. The book title *They Like Jesus but Not the Church* expresses this sentiment well. The church looks too institutional, too much like modernity and its values. Sometimes those who think this way look to Bonhoeffer for support. They use his notion of community in opposition to the church. Community replaces church. This stems from not reading Bonhoeffer aright. It also stems from not quite picking up what he means by "religionless Christianity." This phrase, which causes some consternation among interpreters of Bonhoeffer's thought, will be explored in chapter 7 below.

A sociological look at this phenomenon proves revealing. In a typical new spiritual community, everyone looks pretty much like the next person. Such communities tend not to be multigenerational, but instead end up being monolithic gatherings of progressive twenty- or thirty-somethings united by disaffection for their evangelical or fundamentalist upbringing.

Reflecting on Bonhoeffer's experiences at Bethel, explored in chapter 2 above, we see that the diversity of the congregation in its worship services there impressed him deeply. Even at Finkenwalde, at the underground seminary, Bonhoeffer made sure that the worship services welcomed families from the surrounding villages. He did not want worship services consisting of only the students. They, of course, held chapel at Finkenwalde among themselves. But Bonhoeffer wanted the old to worship alongside of the young, the robust to sing with the weak. Monolithic congregations miss this, and in missing it they miss a great deal. Paul's metaphor of the body drives this point home. A body composed of all elbows would be rather grotesque, not to mention rather useless. So, too, monolithic bodies—peer groups—are not churches in the Pauline sense. The true body of Christ has many, diverse members, some strong, some weak, all different (see 1 Cor. 12:17–19).

And while Bonhoeffer stressed community at Finkenwalde—we could say that at Finkenwalde he literally wrote *the* book on community—he never saw the community he worked so hard to establish there as supplanting the church. He had long harbored suspicions that the typical training of ministers in the German seminaries and universities fell short of preparing ministers for service in the church. Eberhard Bethge, Bonhoeffer's student at Finkenwalde who later became his close prison correspondent, recalls that Bonhoeffer "was convinced that prayer could be taught and learned, yet neither the university faculties nor seminaries included prayer in their curricula."[18] Even more fundamentally, Bonhoeffer sought to correct the absence of concern for one's own spirituality in the course of seminary study. Bethge further speaks of the classes as "a breathtaking surprise," as students "suddenly realized they were not there simply to learn new techniques" and be mere recipients of instruction.[19] Bonhoeffer made sure they would learn. In fact, when he realized they were deficient in their reading and writing skills, he immediately drew up a list of books that he required them to read in their "off time."

In addition to emphasizing a rigorous ministerial education and preparation, Bonhoeffer stressed the person who was being instructed. He cared deeply about the interior spiritual lives of his students. Knowing human nature as well as he did, Bonhoeffer also realized that he could not leave such work to chance. It had to be intentional, and it had to be programmed. Bonhoeffer scheduled it right into the day's activities. He set up Finkenwalde as a corrective to what he had seen gone awry at places like Berlin and the other universities and seminaries. He saw Finkenwalde as a community that would pray together, sing together, suffer together, eat together, work together, and play together. If it was a particularly fine day, Bonhoeffer would cancel classes and off to the woods they would go for a hike, or to the fields with a *fussball*, or as Americans call it, a soccer ball.

So Bonhoeffer indeed stressed community at Finkenwalde, but he also stressed the church. He held church services with preaching and the sacraments and order and liturgy. When he first scouted out the property at Finkenwalde, his priority was to find a room suitable for the Sunday worship service. All of this is to say that when Bonhoeffer speaks of community, he means primarily the church. Those who look back to Bonhoeffer on the topic of community—and he well repays the look—must always be careful not to neglect the church when they return to the present day and speak of and seek to develop communities. For Bonhoeffer, the church is always community, but it's pretty close to the truth to say the opposite: *The community*—the true community Bonhoeffer extols—*is nearly always the church.*

---

[18] Eberhard Bethge, *Dietrich Bonhoeffer: A Biography*, enl. ed. (Minneapolis: Fortress, 2000), 464.
[19] Ibid., 450. Bethge says this particularly of the seminary at Zingst, the temporary home for the underground seminary prior to Finkenwalde.

Please note the word "nearly." When Bonhoeffer writes about community, he *primarily* means the church. We need to be careful that in all of our present-day stressing of community we don't do so at the expense or neglect of the church. But Bonhoeffer does say "nearly always." So while we need caution, we also realize that the church is not *exclusively* what Bonhoeffer meant when he spoke of community. Bonhoeffer stressed the community of peer groups, like the community at Finkenwalde and in earlier such communities as the "Thursday Circle." These, like the church, are genuine communities.

Bonhoeffer began the Thursday Circle in 1927 while in Berlin. This was a group of young men, late teenagers, personally selected by Bonhoeffer. They would meet from 5:25 p.m. until 7:00—one must appreciate Bonhoeffer's sense of precision. They had a prescribed list of topics and Bonhoeffer led, but never commandeered, the conversation. Metaxas explains that Bonhoeffer set up the Thursday Circle because "he felt it vitally important to train up the next generation of young men."[20] One of the Thursday Circle members, Goetz Grosch, would later be Bonhoeffer's student at Finkenwalde. Metaxas records the sad note, however, "Tragically Grosch and most of the young men from the Thursday Circle died during the war, either on the field of battle or" as many of them came from Jewish families, "in concentration camps."[21]

We should not overlook the small circle of community, that of friendship. Probably no friendship of Bonhoeffer's speaks to this more poignantly than that he shared with Eberhard Bethge. The kind of friendship Bonhoeffer and Bethge shared is sadly all too rare. This was the kind of friendship everyone wants, even needs. Bonhoeffer, the elder of the two, was more mentor at first. But as the seasons rolled on and the bond forged, he looked to his friendship with Bethge as refuge. In 1944, Bonhoeffer memorialized their friendship in a poem he simply titled "The Friend." It speaks of the levels of friendship we develop, recalling the days of youth and the playmates who share our childhood adventures "into wondrous, faraway realms."[22] But as we get older and life settles in, our soul "longs for friendship's understanding spirit."[23] And when God graciously grants such a friendship, we treasure it. We treasure it because we need it:

---

[20] Eric Metaxas, *Bonhoeffer: Pastor, Martyr, Prophet, Spy* (Nashville: Thomas Nelson, 2010), 64.
[21] Ibid., 65.
[22] Bonhoeffer, "The Friend," August 28, 1944, *DBWE* 8:528.
[23] Ibid., 529.

Like a fortress, where the spirit returns
after confusion and danger,
finding refuge, comfort, and strength
which is the friend to the friend.[24]

These kinds of community also play a role in our spiritual life. They do not, for Bonhoeffer, replace the church or even take priority over the church. They are a poor substitute for the church. The church is the institution God promises to bless in the pages of the New Testament. And it is our personal connection to the local church that is paramount in our living the Christian life. These communities—part of the church universal—support the church local. When they supplant the church, something crucial is amiss.

The Ghost of Community Past

Bonhoeffer has a large enough view of the church to recognize that it extends far beyond the contemporary horizon. The church that we belong to also encompasses the past. In a lecture outline "Theology and the Congregation," likely written around 1940, Bonhoeffer asks about the value of the theological disciplines for the congregation. He's really asking about the significance, for a congregation, of the seminary curriculum and the courses ministerial students take in seminary. For example, what is the significance of church history for the congregation? Bonhoeffer answers this with a chain of propositions. The congregation must have the Bible and biblical teaching. But, he argues, "One cannot overlook that between us and the Bible there stands a *church* that has a history."[25] Then he immediately writes, "Not Biblicism!"[26]

Bonhoeffer reminds us here that we are a people with a past. The neglect of the past is conspicuous in some places on the current evangelical horizon, the places where biblicism rules the day. This attitude of biblicism, when it comes to spirituality, leads devout and sincere people to think they are better off going it alone. They have the Holy Spirit, they have the Bible, therefore they have all they need for life and godliness—even though the Holy Spirit speaking through the Bible has already revealed that we were made to be in community. Biblicism means more than simply taking the Bible as one's authority.

[24] Ibid., 529.
[25] *DBWE* 16:495.
[26] *DBWE* 16:495.

Even Luther, who spoke so forcefully and loudly of *sola Scriptura*, reminds us of the need for church history and for meaningful connections to our past. In his essay "On the Councils and the Church," Luther indeed argues that the church of previous generations is not a source of authority, since the Bible alone is the church's authority.[27] He clearly finds the Roman Catholic understanding of tradition as authoritative to be patently wrong. Nevertheless, Luther holds the church of previous generations in high regard. In fact, one may rather see him as a reluctant Reformer. Luther's first desire was to reform his church from within. It was only after they kicked him out that he set about forming the church anew in Germany. Tradition may not be the ultimate or final authority. That role belongs exclusively to the Word of God. But tradition does have a degree of authority, and it is certainly useful and instructive. We set tradition aside, Luther argues, at our peril.

This is especially true when it comes to living the Christian life. The Christian community of the past is both useful and instructive for our understanding of the Bible and what it means to be a disciple of Christ. Consider alone what we can learn from Bonhoeffer, a figure from our past. History matters. There is no gap between us and the Bible. Instead, there is a church.

Life Together

Though we briefly sketched out Bonhoeffer's answer to the question of what the church is, we need to further explore his thought on church life. Bonhoeffer provides a vivid, compelling picture of church life in *Life Together*. This book offers the world what Bonhoeffer and his small band of seminarians experienced at Finkenwalde. The Gestapo shut down the seminary in late September 1937. The next summer some of the students met at Zingst. Many from the original group were missing, having been arrested and imprisoned. And after that meeting, Bonhoeffer sat down to write his book, essentially composing it in the month of September 1938.

Bonhoeffer hoped *Life Together* would accomplish a new way of thinking about the church, a way of thinking centered in Christ and resulting in service to others. As Bonhoeffer surveyed the church in his day, he saw both of these lacking, resulting in an emaciated church. With his emphasis on Christ, we are back to Bonhoeffer's starting point of christology, the topic

---

[27] This shorter work by Luther may be found in Timothy Lull and William L. Russell, eds., *Martin Luther's Basic Theological Writings*, 3rd ed. (Minneapolis: Fortress, 2012), 363–85.

of the previous chapter. Geffrey Kelly, the editor of the volume contain-
ing *Life Together* in the collected writings of Bonhoeffer, draws attention to
how the themes of Bonhoeffer's earlier dissertations and thought permeate
this work: "*Life Together* never strays from this form of Christocentrism."[28]
Kelly continues,

> One has only to notice coursing through *Sanctorum Communio* the dy-
> namic reality of Jesus Christ, whose vicarious action in the Christian
> church is the life-giving principle of the visible communion of saints, to
> appreciate the way Bonhoeffer later depicts Jesus' presence inspiriting the
> Christian community in *Life Together*.[29]

To put the matter succinctly, Christ makes community possible. Christ
makes life together possible. Or as Bonhoeffer puts it himself: "Christianity
means community through Jesus Christ and in Jesus Christ. No Christian
community is more or less than this."[30] This is exactly what he already said
back in his dissertation. But here he also has much more new to say. And
here, in *Life Together*, he's fresh from the experiences of Finkenwalde. Those
experiences taught him a great deal about what he already knew to be true.

One of the things experience taught him had to do with our idealistic
notions of church life. We can think glowingly of Christian community, as
if it were some utopian commune. Such notions, Bonhoeffer argues, should
be dismissed as soon as possible. The utopian story goes something like
this. The church is made up of Christians, who have the indwelling Spirit,
have been raised to new life in Christ, have been given new hearts, and
have been given grace upon grace. Consequently, everyone loves everyone
else to the fullest degree. But all too quickly we realize this is not the case.
And so enters disillusionment, confusion, even resentment. In such times
people even go AWOL.

Bonhoeffer calls this a "wish dream," and because of this wish dream
"innumerable times a whole Christian community has broken down."[31]
He then surprises us. Writing of how "God's grace speedily shatters such
dreams," Bonhoeffer adds, "By sheer grace, God will not permit us to live
even for a brief period in a dream world."[32] God in his grace shatters our

---

[28] Introduction, *DBWE* 5:8.
[29] Ibid.
[30] Dietrich Bonhoeffer, *Life Together*, trans. Jon W. Doberstein (New York: Harper, 1954), 21. Rather than
refer to the edition of *Life Together* in the *Dietrich Bonhoeffer Works* set (*DBWE* 5), I will be referring to this
edition, since it is more accessible. Hereafter referred to as *LT*.
[31] *LT*, 26.
[32] *LT*, 26–27.

illusions and dreams of peace and harmony. The church is not a hippy commune or a hipster club. The sooner we come face-to-face with the disillusionment with others and the disillusionment with ourselves, Bonhoeffer adds, the better off we and the church are. There is a realism here that we should appreciate, and a realism that, once grasped, goes a long way in sustaining true and genuine community in the church.

We come to grips with all of our own limitations and weaknesses and besetting sins. And we come to grips with the same in others—even in our leaders and heroes. Then we live in real and not ideal communities. Church is not a wish dream. We also need to jettison our misplaced zeal to see the Christian life as a wish-dream life. The Christian life, like the church, is lived in the real world.

Bonhoeffer offers two means by which we can live in real and not ideal communities: forgiveness and gratitude. We ourselves personally live "in the forgiving love of Jesus."[33] We need to extend the same to our brothers and sisters in Christ. Cultivating thankfulness also helps us look past the difficulties, the petty wrongs, the things that go awry in church life. Now we see why the church is the church *through* Jesus Christ.

Forgiveness is underrated and under-practiced. We do not always get it right. And when we get it wrong, we sometimes desire to save face or to justify our actions. We revert to the classic mechanisms of fight or flight. We possess extraordinary ability to do both. It takes humility to recognize a wrong or a fault, to be repentant, to seek forgiveness, and to make restitution. It also takes work and time.

Gratitude is equally underrated and under-practiced. It too requires humility to say "thank you." Saying "thank you" means one is dependent on the other, that one needs the other. Humility also plays a role in graciously and appropriately accepting the thanks and the gratitude. Bonhoeffer could not be more right in stressing forgiveness—both seeking it and giving it—and stressing gratitude—both offering it and welcoming it—as the two means for authentic community.

Further, forgiveness and gratitude both arc back to the gospel, the center upon which and around which the church community is built. Because the church is *in* Jesus Christ, Bonhoeffer sees the goal of the church to be the same as the goal of the incarnate Christ. Jesus lived and proclaimed the message of salvation. He came to declare reconciliation with God. Then he

---

[33] *LT*, 28.

died on the cross to accomplish it. So Bonhoeffer sees our goal as proclaiming the message of peace with God. In the Christian community we are "bringers of the message of salvation."[34]

Listening

In addition to speaking, which is something we all tend to like to do, we also have other ministries in the church. In *Life Together*, Bonhoeffer titles one of the five chapters "Ministry." Since the book grows out of the Finkenwalde experience and the context of his work with ministerial students, one would expect that Bonhoeffer would be thinking of ministry. He has, however, far more than the clergy in view as his audience. In Bonhoeffer's thinking, every child of God is a minister; all Christians are called to ministry. Bonhoeffer addresses our task of ministry by looking at seven particular ministries in the church.

For Bonhoeffer, ministry is not about power and authority, but service. The word itself, *diakonia*, means service, a word held in high esteem by Bonhoeffer. His list of ministries, then, reflects this fundamental starting point of what ministry is about.

I find his list intriguing both because of the actions that appear on it and because of the order in which the actions appear. The "platform" actions of ministry—the ones that get all of the attention, the ones that supply us with our celebrities (yes, we evangelicals do have them)—come last. He puts *proclaiming* (which is broader than but certainly includes preaching and the pulpit ministry) and *authority* (as in the exercise of pastoral authority) sixth and seventh. Next to last and last are not respectable showings. Consider what he puts in the first five slots:

- the ministry of holding one's tongue
- the ministry of meekness
- the ministry of listening
- the ministry of helpfulness
- the ministry of bearing

Bonhoeffer pegs silence as a self-discipline worthy of highest virtue. He gives the first place to the ministry of *holding one's tongue*. He writes, "Where the discipline of the tongue is practiced right from the beginning,

---

[34] *LT*, 23.

each individual will make a matchless discovery. He will be able to cease from constantly scrutinizing the other person, judging him, condemning him, putting him in his particular place where he can gain ascendency over him."[35] The discovery is even richer: "God did not make this person as I would have made him. . . . Now the other person in the freedom with which he was created, becomes the occasion of joy, whereas before he was only a nuisance and an affliction."[36]

Second on Bonhoeffer's list comes the ministry of *meekness*. Bonhoeffer sees this as key to the whole enterprise of ministry, which is service. "He who would learn to serve must first learn to think little of himself."[37] For this, as with the rest of Bonhoeffer's ecclesiology, he takes us to Christ and the cross. Bonhoeffer continues, "Only he who lives by the forgiveness of his sin in Jesus Christ will rightly think little of himself. He will know that his own wisdom reached the end of its tether when Jesus forgave him."[38] Meekness also requires that we associate with the undesirable and lowly. We naturally resist this, Bonhoeffer concedes. Our natural inclination and our cultural context look to the social stratifications we so often use to esteem or dismiss people. We are all equally sinners, Bonhoeffer reminds us. Elsewhere in his writings he stresses that we are all equally created in the image of God. Meekness leads to "true brotherly service."

The fourth and fifth ministries continue this theme of brotherly service. The fourth is *helpfulness*, which entails even "simple assistance in trifling, external matters."[39] Bonhoeffer challenges us here to "be interrupted by God," to put our plans on hold and to help those who come across our path and need help. Not only are we called to help, but we are also called to *bear one another's burdens* (Gal. 6:2). Again, Christ serves as our model here. He bore our burden, the burden of our sin and rebellion against God. So we bear one another's burdens. Bonhoeffer speaks of it as our duty; in fact, he says, "It is the fellowship of the cross to bear the burden of the other. If one does not experience it, the fellowship he belongs to is not Christian. If any member refuses to bear that burden he denies the law of Christ."[40]

We skipped over the third ministry, the ministry of *listening*. In writing, one rule of thumb is to avoid like the plague the use of clichés, like the

---

[35] *LT*, 92.
[36] *LT*, 93.
[37] *LT*, 94.
[38] *LT*, 95.
[39] *LT*, 99.
[40] *LT*, 101.

two in this sentence. Editors give no reason for their prohibition. It's just the law of the Medes and the Persians (which is usually an acceptable saying). But editors have a point: clichés should be avoided when they are cloying, merely common banalities of homespun wisdom that contribute little substance. But here's a saying that, while admittedly a cliché, has some substance to it: God gave us two ears and one mouth for a reason. Listening—attentive, sympathetic listening—comes far too hard for us. Comparatively, talking comes far too easy. It's the reason James the brother of Jesus had to warn us to be "quick to hear" and "slow to speak" (James 1:19) and not the other way around. Consider what Bonhoeffer has to say about the ministry of listening.

He begins his discussion of the ministry of listening by claiming, "The first service that one owes to others in the fellowship consists in listening to them."[41] Bonhoeffer continues with a convicting observation: "Many people are looking for an ear that will listen. They do not find it among Christians, because these Christians are talking where they should be listening."[42] Not only are opportunities to minister lost, but those who fail to listen to others run an even greater risk. As Bonhoeffer points out, "He who can no longer listen to his brother will soon be no longer listening to God either; he will be doing nothing but prattle in the presence of God too."[43] And as if that weren't enough, Bonhoeffer adds the chilling comment: "This is the beginning of the death of the spiritual life, and in the end there is nothing but spiritual chatter and clerical condescension arrayed in pious words."[44] We have an obligation to listen. Not the "impatient, inattentive listening" we so often offer to people. Instead, "we should listen with the ears of God that we may speak the Word of God."[45]

We do well to pause here and consider for a moment this ministry of listening. It requires no special skills other than the self-discipline of keeping ourselves from talking and keeping ourselves from being distracted. As Bonhoeffer points out, many people simply are looking for someone to hear them, people within the church and people without. To claim to be too busy to listen to them means we have put ourselves over them, regarding ourselves higher than them. It means we have failed to love our neighbor.

Bethge summarized Bonhoeffer's sermons as "startling in their direct-

[41] LT, 97.
[42] LT, 97–98.
[43] LT, 98.
[44] LT, 98.
[45] LT, 99.

ness: they made things clear and they made demands."[46] The same rings true of his discussion of ministry. He makes things related to church life clear, and each of the ministries he identifies makes demands that entail obligations.[47]

Once these first five ministries and their respective obligations are in place, then Bonhoeffer turns to the "platform" ministries. In fact, Bonhoeffer makes the case that without these five ministries the platform ministries, just like the preaching in the opening scenes of his novel, become little more than the bellowing of hot air. In *Life Together* Bonhoeffer prefers the expression "empty words." "Then where the ministry of listening, active helpfulness, and bearing with others is faithfully performed, the ultimate and highest service can also be rendered, namely, the ministry of the Word of God."[48] This statement deserves a little unpacking. First, Bonhoeffer stresses the need for authentic Christian living before the action of proclamation. To put this colloquially, one needs to walk the walk. Second, Bonhoeffer stresses the primacy of proclamation. Again, putting it colloquially, one *must* talk the talk.

The church is not the church, and Christian community is not genuinely Christian, without the clear, consistent, and conspicuous proclamation of the Word of God. Some currents of evangelicalism today, in their efforts to stress the service ministries, undercut the proclamation of the Word. That's a dangerous trajectory which leads the church away from her moorings and from her unique task in the world. Conversely, some currents in evangelicalism, while faithfully proclaiming the Word of God, undercut the service ministries. The gospel they proclaim falls on deaf or absent ears because they lack the credibility that comes from genuine and active caring. That too is a dangerous trajectory. Bonhoeffer's list of seven ministries, his ordering of the list, and his admonitions regarding the seven ministries on the list could go a long way in correcting these two faulty approaches.

The church, as we continue to learn from Bonhoeffer, is a complex organism. To use another metaphor, the church is like an engine that fires on many pistons. When all pistons fire, it runs like a charm. When they don't, it coughs and spurts its way along and is in desperate need of a mechanic.

---

[46] Bethge, *Dietrich Bonhoeffer*, 444.

[47] For more on Bonhoeffer's sermons, see *The Collected Sermons of Dietrich Bonhoeffer*, ed. Isabel Best (Minneapolis: Fortress, 2012), a collection of sermons drawn from the volumes in the *DBWE*. Best offers an introductory chapter exploring Bonhoeffer as pastor and the importance of his sermons. Each sermon has a brief discussion of the setting. This reader is the best collection available, offering sermons from throughout Bonhoeffer's lifetime.

[48] *LT*, 103.

The connection between this discussion of multi-orbed ministry and the Christian life comes down to this: as the church goes, so go I. There is no isolated Christian life. All of the seven ministries have one thing in common: each requires other people. We cannot conceive of the Christian life, of biblical spirituality, apart from our life together in the church. Further, what leads to a healthy church also leads to a healthy spirituality.

People Are Exhausting

It is comforting to know that the same person who wrote *Life Together* also once said, "I find people extremely exhausting."[49] This is a reality check in the challenging discussion of the demands upon us as we live together. Christ himself set the model by withdrawing from time to time from the crowds, from the disciples, from people—extremely exhausting people.

Bonhoeffer speaks of this in the chapter "The Day Alone." There is a place for solitude and silence. Our contemporary world is not one for solitude and silence. We are a people known, above all, for our distractions. French philosopher, mathematician, and rather wise Christian Blaise Pascal observed, "I have often said that the sole cause of man's unhappiness is that he does not know how to stay quietly in his room."[50]

We are the culture of the iPod, with buds in our ears. We have little tolerance and fortitude for silence. But silence is necessary for us, and it's even necessary for community.

By silence, Bonhoeffer does not mean mindless meditation. Instead, "Silence is the simple stillness of the individual under the Word of God."[51] Bonhoeffer actually dismisses the mystical desires of "getting beyond the word." We honor and receive the Word when we are silent before it, truly listening to it. In addition to this private and silent meditation on the Word of God, we also spend the day alone in "private prayer and intercession."[52] We'll return to each of these spiritual disciplines (reading the Word, prayer, and intercession) in chapters 4 and 5 below. For now, we should hear the words of Bonhoeffer, "Let him who cannot be alone beware of community," which he follows up with, "Let him who is not in community beware of being alone."[53]

---

[49] Bonhoeffer to Maria von Wedemeyer, December 1, 1943, *LPP*, 417.
[50] Pascal, *Pensées* 139, quoted in "Addicted to Diversion and Afraid of Silence," http://thegospelcoalition .org/blogs/justintaylor/2011/08/26/addicted-to-diversion-and-afraid-of-silence.
[51] *LT*, 79.
[52] *LT*, 81.
[53] *LT*, 77.

Conclusion: Lord, What Would You Have Me to Do?

At one point or another, all of us wrestle with the question of what to do with our lives. Because we know as Christians that what we do now has eternal consequences, this question becomes all the more pressing. The question sometimes takes the form, what's God's will for my life? Sometimes we ask whether we should pursue full-time Christian ministry. Sometimes lay people wrestle with the significance of their work. Sometimes high school and college students and twenty-somethings (twenty-seven is the new eighteen, right?) wrestle with the myriad choices before them. Sometimes, perhaps more often than not, such questions stymie us. They hold us back rather than spur us on.

If Bonhoeffer were to meet a person with such questions he would say: Do something. Serve somebody. That is ministry. That is God's will. Certainly there is legitimacy to taking stock and being strategic and asking soul-searching questions. There's also a place for waiting on God, for times of withdrawal and personal meditation. But sometimes we overthink it, and sometimes we overindulge the self. Bonhoeffer lists seven ministries in *Life Together*. All of us can do at least one of them well, many can do a few of them well, and even a few gifted individuals in the church can do them all well. In other words, we can all do something. We are all called to ministry.

This question of God's will also extends, at times, to our church connections. It's easy to see faults and find fault. Our consumer culture has conditioned us to view everything in our lives like, well, consumers. We can even think of our church connections like consumers, shopping for the most convenient option that brings the most self-fulfillment. Bonhoeffer reminds us that since the church is made of people, who happen to be sinners, it can be messy and inconvenient and feel unfulfilling. Thinking like a consumer when it comes to the church robs us of genuine Christian community. Community—which at its foundational and essential nature is composed of other people—consists of burdens and suffering, challenges and difficulties. None of these makes for good advertising. But you bond the deepest with those you suffer with.

Community that is genuine allows the Word of God to rule freely. Like the plane in the hands of a skilled carpenter, that Word cuts across us, knocks off our hard edges, and conforms and shapes us for use. This fails to make for good advertising, too. We like our personal freedom and our personal sovereignty over our lives. But in community we are called to submit—to the Word and to others. Ultimately we submit to the one who is Lord of all (see Rom. 6:17–22 and the freedom that Paul celebrates as a slave to righteousness).

When we are robbed of genuine Christian community, we are robbed of genuine Christian living. To put the matter positively, when we experience genuine Christian community (our life together) we experience genuine Christian living (our life alone). That is why ecclesiology is at the center of Bonhoeffer's theology, and at the center of his theology of the Christian life. The Christian life is lived in community, the community of the church that exists "in and through Jesus Christ."

PART 3

DISCIPLINES

This is very important. Jesus tells us that when you want to pray to God, think first of all about God. Leave yourselves completely aside for a moment and see how much more important it is that we first learn to say: your name, your kingdom, your will. First you, and again you. Your name and not mine, your will and not mine.

DIETRICH BONHOEFFER,
INSTRUCTIONS ON THE LORD'S
PRAYER TO HIS CATECHISM CLASS,
BERLIN, 1930

How can we do all this if we are not basically grateful human beings?

DIETRICH BONHOEFFER,
SERMON ON I THESSALONIANS 5:16–18,
TELTOW, 1930

CHAPTER 4

WORD

Those who have accepted God's Word must begin to seek God; they can do no other.

DIETRICH BONHOEFFER,
MEDITATIONS ON PSALM 119, 1939

I read, meditate, write, pace up and down my cell—without rubbing myself sore against the walls like a polar bear. . . . I am reading the Bible straight through from cover to cover.

DIETRICH BONHOEFFER,
FROM TEGEL PRISON, 1943

A tempest in a teacup rages over who best lays claim to Dietrich Bonhoeffer. On the one hand, those of a more liberal persuasion are convinced he belongs solely to them. On the other hand, theological conservatives plant their own flag over his legacy. Which one is right? To put it pointedly, is Bonhoeffer an evangelical?

While this debate has been around for some time, Eric Metaxas's extremely popular biography served to stir the pot in more recent moments. Metaxas, both in his book and in interviews, has beat the drum of Bonhoeffer's conservative credentials. Metaxas states that Bonhoeffer does not look like a liberal. Some from the Bonhoeffer "guild," the academics who populate the International Bonhoeffer Society and carry on the task of translation and scholarly interaction with his work, have shot back. They argue that this is a clear case of finding what you're looking for. One scholar goes so far as to suggest that Metaxas's biography be retitled *Bonhoeffer: Hijacked*. In other words, Metaxas set out to find a theologically conservative, evangelical-approved Bonhoeffer, and Metaxas found enough to make one.

Surprisingly (or maybe not so), the right wing of evangelicalism also went after Bonhoeffer, and Metaxas's take on him. They cited Bonhoeffer's "religionless Christianity" theme, his ecumenical efforts (Bonhoeffer even admired Gandhi!), and—the trump card—Bonhoeffer's relationship with Karl Barth. All of this is proof enough, this group avers, not to have him in the fold.

The "religionless Christianity" has consistently been a bone of contention when it comes to evangelical estimations of Bonhoeffer. Take, for example, Earl Cairns's textbook *Christianity through the Centuries*. Cairns squarely, but wrongly, puts Bonhoeffer in the "God Is Dead" camp.[1] Cairns also notes, "Dietrich Bonhoeffer (1906–45), who had been influenced by Barth and Bultmann, spoke of man as having 'come of age' intellectually."[2] Cairns rather unfortunately fails to see how Bonhoeffer was critiquing this coming of age, not commending it—as the "God Is Dead" theologians were. Bonhoeffer's "religionless Christianity" was ultimately a debilitating salvo against the very liberalism Cairns claims him to be a part of—not to mention Bonhoeffer's criticism of both Barth and (especially) Bultmann. Bonhoeffer has been given, and still gets, a reputation he doesn't at all deserve.

Nevertheless, the debate continues. What is the significance of this debate over whether Bonhoeffer belongs to liberals or conservatives? One answer would be "not much." We could, if we wanted to, debate any number of figures from church history and which team they would be on. Luther had significant difficulties with Augustine over Augustine's lack of clarity on imputation. Some have pointed to John Wycliffe's lack of clarity on justification. And what do we make of most of the theologians and churchmen from the Middle Ages? Consider the range of opinion among contemporary evangelicals on Thomas Aquinas alone. We need to be careful in these

---

[1] The "God Is Dead" theologians, such as Thomas J. J. Altizer, argued that a transcendent God, or even transcendence itself, was no longer tenable. Instead they pointed to a fully immanent religious expression. Christianity is nothing more than sociology or anthropology to the "God Is Dead" theologians. Such was their popularity that *Time* magazine devoted an issue to the matter. The cover of the April 8, 1966, edition rather ominously asked, "Is God Dead?"

[2] Earl E. Cairns, *Christianity Through the Centuries: A History of the Christian Church*, 3rd ed. (Grand Rapids: Zondervan, 1996), 465.

debates over who gets to claim whom, so that we not do injustice to these figures in their own contexts.

But another answer to the question of the significance of this debate would be that a great deal is at stake. If being a theological conservative means having an orthodox view of Christ and his work, believing that Christ is the God-man who alone provides redemption through his atoning work on the cross, and holding to a high view of Scripture as God's only authoritative Word, then the camp to which Bonhoeffer belongs makes all the difference. As J. Gresham Machen, the champion of theological conservatism in the face of American liberalism, argued so eloquently and forcefully in *Christianity and Liberalism* (1925), you are free to deny a high view of Christ and his work, and you are even free to deny a high view of the Bible. But you cannot deny such beliefs and at the same time call it Christianity. You are no more free to do that than you are free to create square circles—it's a contradiction in terms.

Bonhoeffer's theological conservative *bona fides* matter a great deal. If his theology is wrong, then he is not a sure guide for living the Christian life. If his theology is askew, then his theology of spirituality is simply not to be trusted as a model for us. "Orthopraxy" flows from orthodoxy. An isolated "orthopraxy" is tenuous indeed.

We have already seen in chapter 2 how Bonhoeffer's orthodox christology results in a robust basis for living the Christian life. In this chapter we will see how his orthodox view of Scripture also results in a firm foundation for living the Christian life. His view of Scripture, though, moves us far from a foundational investigation into the nature of spirituality. His view of Scripture leads us right from theory (theology and doctrine) to practice, to the spiritual discipline of reading the Bible. And his practice of reading the Bible leads us right to obeying God and living as disciples of Christ.

Christians are people of the Book. We have, for good or for ill, our gurus, our leaders, our seminars, and our techniques. But at the end of the day, we must return to and live from a book, *the Book*. Any theology of the Christian life, any spirituality, must always trace back to and derive from Scripture. The lifeblood of the Christian life is God's Word to us. It alone abides, while everything else—our techniques, our seminars, our leaders, our gurus—fades and falls and passes.

Bonhoeffer should not be counted among theological liberals. He was a theological conservative. He not only had an orthodox view of Christ; he also prominently displayed that view in his work and placed it at the center of his thought and life. He held to the doctrine of justification by faith, and he had a high view of Scripture. Bonhoeffer believed the Bible to be the Word of God, he submitted to God's Word, and he took God's Word and its claims on his life seriously—a life-and-death level of seriousness. Those three doctrines—christology, justification by faith alone, and the authority of Scripture—constitute conservative theological orthodoxy. Bonhoeffer facilely passes the test.

We can even lay claim to Bonhoeffer as an evangelical. David Bebbington's "quadrilateral" offers a widely accepted definition of evangelicalism. Bebbington sees biblicism[3] (a high view of Scripture, seeing the Bible as God's Word), crucicentrism (a focus on Christ's atoning death on the cross), conversionism (a focus on the new birth and belief that sinful human beings must be converted), and activism (the living out of the gospel in works) as defining marks of evangelicalism.[4] All four may be found in Bonhoeffer. The activism is plainly there throughout his life.

As for conversionism, Bonhoeffer clearly held to justification by faith and the necessity of the preaching of Christ and his cross work for conversion. In his draft of "What Do We Learn from the Mission to the Non-Christians?," written while at Tegel, Bonhoeffer notes, "Mission not out of pity for the 'poor heathen' . . . but they do not have *Christ*. Thus not primarily not out of *pity*, but because Christ *must* be preached (I Cor. 9:16) *anagke*, a command."[5] Near the end of his life, he himself could take comfort in knowing, "My sins are covered by the forgiving love of Christ crucified."[6] Bonhoeffer's crucicentrism is on display in such works as his "Lectures on Christology," with their crescendo that our only hope is in the atoning death of the God-man, Christ. The case for Bonhoeffer's high view of Scripture follows below.

We need to appreciate Bonhoeffer's theological affirmations beyond their soundness, however. We need to see how his affirmations led to prac-

---

[3] The biblicism referred to here is not the same as that decried by Bonhoeffer in the previous chapter. Bebbington's term speaks to the authority of the Bible. What Bonhoeffer decried was a biblicism that has room for the Bible only, and not for the office of teacher, for denominations and confessions, or for church history and tradition.
[4] David Bebbington, *Evangelicalism in Modern Britain: A History from the 1730s to the 1980s*, rev. ed. (Oxford: Routledge, 1989). Church historians have made a (minor) cottage industry out of arguing over the "Bebbington quadrilateral," but those debates tend to hover around starting points for evangelicalism. When it comes to giving criteria for who is and who is not an evangelical, since there is no ecclesiastical body charged with overseeing it, the "Bebbington quadrilateral" tends to serve quite well.
[5] *DBWE* 16:498. The Greek word means obligation.
[6] Bonhoeffer to Eberhard Bethge, August 23, 1944, *LPP*, 393.

tice. We need to see how he lived based on what he believed. If we let him, his thoughts on Scripture and his practice of Bible reading will most certainly challenge and convict us not only to affirm with our mouths that we are "people of the Book" who have a high view of Scripture, but also to live that affirmation with our whole being.

Bonhoeffer's Conversion to the Bible

While I have asserted Bonhoeffer's theological conservatism, it is true that he grew up in a context of liberalism. One of his professors was the influential liberal historian and theologian Adolf von Harnack. The schools he attended took higher criticism as a given—the Bible was not so much a divine revelation as it was a human reflection on the human-divine relationship. Liberalism even coursed through Bonhoeffer's bloodline. Karl August von Hase, Bonhoeffer's maternal great-grandfather, taught church history and theology, wrote books, and was patently liberal.

Bonhoeffer, though, went in a different direction. Reflecting back on his formative years in theological training, he wrote of his discovery of the Bible as if it were his conversion: "Then something happened, something that has changed and transformed my life to the present day. For the first time I discovered the Bible."[7] Once Bonhoeffer discovered the Bible, he read it. His reading of the Bible, which for him meant necessarily taking its claims seriously, led him to the life he lived. Eventually it led him—as he understood his obedience to its claims on his life—to his martyrdom.

We need to first look at Bonhoeffer's doctrine of Scripture, since his understanding of revelation is crucial to his christology and his ecclesiology—those two foundational pillars of the Christian life. After such a look at his theology of Scripture, we will turn to his practice of reading the Bible. Bonhoeffer was by trade a churchman, a pastor. Consequently, he has a great deal to say about the pastor and his Bible and about the role of the sermon in the life of the believer. Finally, we'll look at his practice of reading and meditating upon God's Word.

Bonhoeffer's Doctrine of Scripture

As a nineteen-year-old in a doctoral seminar on systematic theology, Dietrich could write, or better, confess, "Revelation for us can be found only

---

[7] Cited in Eberhard Bethge, *Dietrich Bonhoeffer: A Biography*, enl. ed. (Minneapolis: Fortress, 2000), 205.

in Scripture"; and to someone who would ask why such is the case, he has a ready answer: "This is where God speaks and this is where it pleases God to be personally revealed."[8] He makes a forceful point earlier in the same essay: "Christian religion stands or falls with the belief in a historical and perceptibly real divine revelation."[9] When the tables turned and Bonhoeffer became the professor, he said the exact same thing. In his lectures at Berlin in 1931 and 1932, he insisted, "Absoluteness is grounded not in a religious experience, but rather in the word of God."[10]

Though I have argued in chapters 2 and 3 that christology and ecclesiology are at the center of Bonhoeffer's theology—noting that some have even called the pair a Christo-ecclesiology—it wouldn't be far from the mark to say that revelation actually forms the center. Bonhoeffer himself argued for as much in his doctoral dissertation, *Sanctorum Communio*. The incarnate Christ is in fact *the* revelation of God, as John's prologue has it (John 1:1–18). The church then is also the revelation of God in the world. Though the exact reason why may confound us, God has chosen the church, his people, as the means by which he makes himself and the message of redemption and reconciliation in Christ known.

The connection between the church and revelation, though, runs deeper still. Bonhoeffer writes in his first dissertation (putting the whole sentence in italics), *"Only the concept of revelation can lead to the Christian concept of the church."*[11] He sees Christ as in fact the center revelation. Bonhoeffer makes a play on the Greek word for church, *ekklēsia*, which means "the called out." That act of calling out the church, Bonhoeffer would have us see, speaks to the divine origin of revelation and the divine origin of the church. The church is called into existence by God. But then Bonhoeffer makes a distinct turn in his doctrine of revelation, a concrete turn distancing himself from theological liberalism. This turn consists of Bonhoeffer's view of the Bible as a depository, as it were, of God's revealed will, ways, and truth. And it is a revelation that is authoritative and historically reliable.

This last paragraph may need some explanation. There were two opposing sides in the German world of theological and biblical studies from the nineteenth through the mid-twentieth centuries. There were, on the one hand, the naturalists or historicists. This side denied the divine origin

---

[8] *DBWE* 9:289.
[9] *DBWE* 9:285.
[10] Bonhoeffer, "The History of Twentieth-Century Systematic Theology," *DBWE* 11:209.
[11] *DBWE* 1:134.

of Christianity and of Christian Scripture. Liberalism, on the other hand, countered by stressing the divine origin. But they so stressed that divine origin that they ended up running right past (or better, through) the Scriptures to a dynamic God who *speaks*. Liberalism would not be bound by a book or bind God to a book. These two sides dominated the German scene. Bonhoeffer's view of Scripture sidesteps both erroneous views. He saw that the Bible is the authoritative Word of God, not that one has to look through it or past it to get to God's Word.

The clearest expression of Bonhoeffer's doctrine of Scripture may likely be found in the Bethel Confession of 1933. There are actually three versions of the confession. The first, typically referred to as the first draft, was written over the spring and summer of 1933 by Bonhoeffer and Hermann Sasse. The second draft, written in August and thus called the August Version, also saw Wilhelm Vischer contribute. There is very little difference between these two drafts beyond stylistic issues and wordsmithery. The third draft is referred to as the November Version. This version had a lot more hands working on it. The editorial process frustrated Bonhoeffer, who by then was in London. He saw the original "spoiled" by these editors and rejected the changes. When a published copy did reach Bonhoeffer, he wrote on it, "Too many cooks spoil the broth. An anonymous author. D.B."[12] By adding his initials he pretty much signed away his claim to anonymity.

The committee represented a spectrum of views, not all as theologically conservative as Bonhoeffer's. The changes here were not merely stylistic. They were substantive. Consequently, Bonhoeffer altogether abandoned the project he had started. Both Sasse and Vischer took the same path as Bonhoeffer.

The change from the earlier two drafts to the November Version is nowhere more acutely felt than the first article of the Bethel Confession, concerning the doctrine of Scripture. Consider these two sentences from the first draft and the August Version over against the sentences from the November Version, noting the italicized difference:

Early Version by Bonhoeffer

The Holy Scriptures of the Old and New Testaments are the sole source and norm for the doctrine of the church. *They constitute the fully valid witness*, authenticated by the Holy Spirit, that Jesus of Nazareth . . .

---

[12] *DBWE* 12:513.

November Version by Committee
Holy Scripture, the Old and New Testament, is the only source and norm
of the church's doctrine. It attests, *valid in its unity*, that the same Jesus
of Nazareth . . .[13]

It is one thing to say that Scripture is a "fully valid witness." It is another to see it as "valid in its unity." This latter means nothing more than
Scripture coheres with reference to itself, that Scripture is coherent. Coherence is an admirable quality, to be sure, but one that stops short of a
clear articulation of an orthodox view of Scripture. There is an objective
dimension to declaring that Scripture is "fully valid." The statement by
Bonhoeffer says more about Scripture than its self-referential coherence.
Bonhoeffer's statement affirms Scripture to be true.

When it comes to the doctrine of Scripture (or any doctrine, for that
matter), clarity, directness, and forcefulness are always better than ambiguity or equivocation. Theodore Roosevelt almost made a career out of
castigating journalists or political opponents who used "weasel words."
Theologians under the authority of God's Word will renounce such "dis-
graceful, underhanded ways" and instead practice an "open statement of
the truth" (2 Cor. 4:2).

Consider below the fuller statement of Bonhoeffer on Scripture from
the first draft:

The Holy Scriptures of the Old and New Testaments are the sole source
and norm for the doctrine of the church. They constitute the fully valid
witness, authenticated by the Holy Spirit, that Jesus of Nazareth, who
was crucified under Pontius Pilate, is the Christ, Israel's Messiah, the
anointed King of the Church, the Son of the living God. Everything the
church teaches must be measured solely by this guiding principle of the
Holy Scriptures and be revealed as pure doctrine through it alone. The
Holy Scriptures alone witness to the divine revelation, which occurred
as a one-time, unrepeatable and self-contained history of salvation. We
know about this history only from the prophetic and apostolic words of
the Old and New Testaments, and the church can proclaim the revela-

---

[13] Bethel Confession, published in *DBWE* 12:375. The August Version has "valid in its entirety" for the
key phrase. Only the Early Version and the August Version appear in the English edition of *Dietrich Bonhoeffer Works*. The November Version is available (in German) in the German edition of the *Works*. The
only English version to date may be found at http://www.lutheranwiki.org/The_Bethel_Confession:_
November_Version. For a brief sketch of the history of these drafts of the Bethel Confession, see Carsten
Nicolaisen, "Concerning the History of the Bethel Confession," in *DBWE*, 12:509–13.

tion only by interpreting this Word that bears witness to it. The facts of salvation history to which the Scriptures bear witness (i.e. the election of Israel and the condemnation of its sin, the revelation of the Law of Moses, the incarnation, the teachings and deeds of Jesus Christ, his death on the cross and his resurrection, the founding of the church) are unique revelatory acts of God, which the church has to proclaim as such and as valid also for us today.[14]

The Bible is the record of the divine activity in human history, in real history. The Bible records these events as "facts," as objective events that occurred in space and time. Because the Bible is the exclusive witness to divine revelation, it alone holds the place of authority in the church. Nothing else supplants it. This view distances Bonhoeffer from both the historicists and the liberals.

The statement continues to list rejections, all in the service of clarifying the differences between a high view of Scripture as held by Bonhoeffer and a lower view of Scripture all too prevalent in the national church. In short, Bonhoeffer argues that we must submit to the text, the living and active Word of God. We err when we submit the text to our preferences and predilections. So he confesses:

We reject the false doctrine that tears apart the unity of the Holy Scriptures, that claims to separate God's words from human words for its own arbitrary reasons. The unity of the entire Holy Scriptures is Jesus Christ, the Crucified and Risen One, who speaks throughout the Scriptures wherever and whenever he wants. We are not the judges of God's Word in the Bible; instead, the Bible is given to us so that through it we may submit ourselves to Christ's judgment. Only the Spirit hears the Word of God from the Bible.[15] But this Spirit itself comes to us only through the words of the Holy Scriptures in their entirety, and therefore can never, except by enthusiasm [*Schwärmerei*], be separated from these words.

We reject the false doctrine that consults the Scriptures only as an historical document that gives examples of certain generally valid truths.

---

[14] *DBWE* 12:375.
[15] The phrase "God's word in the Bible" is likely owing to Barth's influence. The difference between Karl Barth and Dietrich Bonhoeffer, though, is that Bonhoeffer makes room for the concreteness of Scripture, which Barth's theology lacks. Barth's lack of concreteness leads him to a view of redemption that comes pretty close to universalism. A theologian friend of mine once referred to Barth's view of redemption as "incipient universalism." Friends of Barth don't like the charge—but it sticks. Barth is also, in the immortal phrase of Margaret Thatcher, "wobbly" on the historical Adam. Bonhoeffer is not. Bonhoeffer's more concrete view of revelation, his view that the Bible is God's word, leads him to a concrete view of redemption. Bonhoeffer describes it as "fact." And therein lies the key difference between Barth and Bonhoeffer.

It is a denial of the uniqueness and the historicity of God's revelation to draw conclusions about the election of any other people, or perhaps of all peoples, from the election of Israel as God's chosen people, or to conclude from God's giving the Law of Moses to Israel that the laws of all nations are given to them by God. The saving acts of God in the Bible are significant not as examples or symbols, but rather as subjects of the church's proclamation of the unique revelation of God.[16]

As these rejections attest, Bonhoeffer held to a high view of Scripture. He clearly distanced himself from his liberal context, and he clearly put himself *under* God's Word as the authority for the church and for life. When Bonhoeffer speaks of how wrongheaded it would be to deduce from the election of Israel the "maxim" that God elects other nations as chosen, he's referring to his own nation. Hitler looked for and got from the church divine blessing on the Third Reich. It's chilling to think of how the church lent credibility to Hitler. It's far more chilling to think of the consequences of what Hitler did because of it. The stakes here could not have been higher. Bonhoeffer, in writing the Bethel Confession, was a theologian in service of the church.

Bonhoeffer's high view of Scripture also comes through in his criticism of more liberal views in his own day. During his second visit to New York he kept a diary. On June 22, 1939, according to his diary, he spent the morning writing and the afternoon reading. He was reading Reinhold Niebuhr's *Interpretation of Christian Ethics*. Bonhoeffer was not impressed by the book, referring to its "wrong and superficial statements," then adding a cryptic, but stinging criticism: "'myth' instead of the Word of God."[17] So he drilled right to the core of Niebuhr's deficiency, that of a too-low view of the Bible. By labeling the Bible "myth," Niebuhr could then sift through it for that which represented the eternal truth. Bonhoeffer thought differently. He saw the Bible as God's Word, as standing over and above him.

Later, while in prison, Bonhoeffer would address the mythological view head on. This time he would have Rudolph Bultmann in view. Bultmann held the New Testament to have accommodated a mythological worldview. The New Testament authors expressed their understanding of Christ in mythological terms. Bultmann then sought to get at the eternal truths encapsulated within the myth. The package, the biblical text itself, can go, but

---

[16] *DBWE* 12:378–79.
[17] Bonhoeffer, "American Diary," June 22, 1939, *DBWE* 15:229.

the eternal truth nestled in it must stay, held Bultmann. He applied this to the record of miracles in the New Testament and even to the miracle of the resurrection of Christ.

Bonhoeffer did not want to see Bultmann's view take hold of the ministers in the Confessing Church. In a letter from prison to Bethge, Bonhoeffer offered his counter to Bultmann's view: "My view is that the full content, including the 'mythological' concepts, must be kept—the New Testament is not a mythological clothing of a universal truth; this mythology (resurrection, etc.) is the thing itself."[18] This recalls what Bonhoeffer wrote in the Bethel Confession concerning Christ: "The cross of Jesus Christ is not at all a symbol of anything, it is rather the unique revelatory act of God."[19]

Exactly one month later, Bonhoeffer was still thinking of the low view of Scripture by his fellow German theologians and scholars. This time he was writing in response to Paul Tillich, who had expatriated to America during the War. To Tillich, and to the host of liberal theologians, Bonhoeffer puts it directly: "The Word of God is far removed from this revolt of mistrust, this revolt from below. On the contrary it reigns."[20] For Bonhoeffer, God's Word reigns.

The doctrine of Scripture stands as the first domino in a long chain. If we start where Bonhoeffer starts, with the Bible as God's Word standing over us and calling for our submission to it, then the dominos will fall in a certain direction. If, however, we start with the Bible in submission to us and to our predilections, then the dominos fall in an entirely different direction. And as goes our theology, so goes our discipleship and understanding of the Christian life. Again, the differences between Bonhoeffer and liberalism plainly display themselves.

These were not merely theological affirmations for Bonhoeffer. As we'll see below, he also lived his doctrine of Scripture, and he lived it with the same clarity, directness, and forcefulness with which he affirmed it. We'll first see the doctrine of Scripture he taught his students, which he did in both theory and practice.

The Pastor and His Bible

Bonhoeffer studied at the University of Berlin and Union Seminary in New York, and he visited numerous seminaries and even monasteries in Ger-

---

[18] Bonhoeffer to Eberhard Bethge, June 8, 1944, *LPP*, 329.
[19] Bonhoeffer, drafts of Bethel Confession, *DBWE* 12:398.
[20] Bonhoeffer to Eberhard Bethge, July 8, 1944, *LPP*, 346.

many, across Europe, and in Great Britain. However, he didn't always like what he saw. He especially found troubling his own country's tendency to leave the interior lives of ministers out of the course of ministerial training. His time with the underground seminaries in the service of the Confessing Church, first at Zingst, then at Finkenwalde, provided him the opportunity to strike off on a different path.

The real difference at Bonhoeffer's seminaries over against other places was not so much the *curriculum*—though it had differences too. The real difference concerned the *ethos*. Bonhoeffer firmly believed that pastors were called to preach the Word so that people would be brought under conviction of the Word, which would result in their submission and obedience to the Word. Before a pastor could take up such preaching, however, the process had to be true in his own life. The Bible would be at the center of all that happened at Zingst and at Finkenwalde. "The Bible forms the focal point of our work," Bonhoeffer wrote of Finkenwalde, adding, "It has once again become for us the starting point and the center for our theological work and all our Christian action."[21]

That ethos, though, did trickle down to the curriculum. As part of the homiletics course, the course in which would-be pastors were taught how to preach, Bonhoeffer treated his students to lectures on the pastor and the Bible. His student Bethge explains that Bonhoeffer used these lectures to trace out for students how the Bible moves from their own life to the pulpit: the pastor starts with Scripture at the kneeling bench in prayerful meditation, then on the desk for rigorous exegetical study, and then in the pulpit where it is brought forth before a needy people.[22] Most homiletics classes start right with preaching. Bonhoeffer knew some prior work was in order.

Bonhoeffer did pass along practical advice to his students, as well. Bethge summarizes some such advice:

> Write your sermon in daylight; do not write it all at once; "in Christ" there is no room for conditional clauses; the first minutes of the pulpit are the most favorable, so do not waste them with generalities but confront the congregation straight off with the core of the matter; extemporaneous preaching can be done by anyone who really knows the Bible.[23]

---

[21] Bonhoeffer, "A Greeting from the Finkenwalde Seminary," cited in *The Way to Freedom: Letters, Lectures, and Notes, 1935–1939*, ed. Edwin H. Robertson (New York: Harper & Row, 1966), 35.
[22] Bethge, *Dietrich Bonhoeffer*, 442.
[23] Ibid., 443.

Bonhoeffer also favored short sermons, if his sermon manuscripts are any indication. Not long on ornamentation, Bonhoeffer went for directness. "They made things clear," Bethge recalls of Bonhoeffer's sermons, "and they made demands."[24] And that is precisely why Bonhoeffer spent time with his students, future pastors, on their own relationships to the Bible. Before they could stand behind a pulpit and declare the Bible's demands for the congregations, they needed to come to grips with those demands on their own lives.

Perhaps we learn most about Bonhoeffer's impact on these would-be pastors by listening to one. Here is Bethge's testimony on meditation and the pastoral office:

> Because I am a preacher of the Word, I cannot expound Scripture unless I let it speak to me every day. I will misuse the Word in my office if I do not keep meditating on it in prayer. If the Word is often empty to me in the daily office, if I no longer experience it, that should be an unmistakable sign that for a long time I have stopped letting it speak to me. I offend in my office if each day I do not look for the word that my Lord would say to me on that day.[25]

First comes meditation, then comes preaching.

How to Listen to a Sermon: Bonhoeffer's Practice of Preaching

I recently took up distance running as a hobby. A friend of mine once said he took it up too—then put it down very quickly. Like most new to running, I went out too far, too fast, and hurt myself. I took a few days off, tried to run again, felt fine initially, then hurt myself again. On the second time through this cycle, the thought dawned on me that I had no idea what I was doing. I went to see an expert, a physical therapist specializing in sports medicine. He diagnosed the problem, set out a plan, and got me back to running. The moral of the story? We often need experts. We don't have all the answers in our own heads.

God has decreed for his church to have such skilled and gifted guides, as is evidenced in his giving us the office of pastor. Bonhoeffer, as he made so clear in the Bethel Confession, sees the Word of God as the means for our sanctification, our means for growing in grace. Following Reformers

---

[24] Ibid., 444.
[25] Bethge, "Introduction to Daily Meditation," cited in Robertson, *The Way to Freedom*, 57.

like Martin Luther and John Calvin, he actually called Scripture a means of grace. He further understood that the Word, this fount of grace, comes to us in two forms: preaching and prayerful, meditative reading of the Bible. Experts proclaim to us the Word, which we ourselves read.

Bonhoeffer once told his ministerial students that they should "not defend God's Word, but testify to it." He said, "Trust to the Word. It is a ship loaded to the very limits of its capacity."[26] Because the Bible is God's Word, Bonhoeffer had full confidence in it. He knew that as a preacher he had one task in the pulpit, to proclaim God's Word.

In one of his London sermons, Bonhoeffer tells his own congregation, "There is really only one question for a congregation to ask of its pastor: Is he offering us the eternal word of God, the word of life, wherever he can, in the pulpit and in daily life? Or is he giving us stones instead of bread?"[27] When a member of a congregation comes into a church, he should say (though maybe not out loud), "Give us bread that fills our hungry souls!"[28] Bonhoeffer explains what happens when such bread is given. We meet with God, "while the busy world outside sees nothing and knows nothing."[29] He continues, "Out there they are all running after the latest sensations, the excitements of evening in the big city, never knowing that the real sensation, something infinitely more exciting is happening in here: here, where eternity and time meet, where the immortal God receives mortal human beings."[30] That's how Bonhoeffer told his own congregation to listen to his own sermons.

How to Read the Bible: Bonhoeffer's Practice of Reading Scripture

In addition to the preaching of and listening to sermons, there is also the private reading of the Word. Here, too, Bonhoeffer has much to say. We call it *hermeneutics*, the art and science of interpreting the Bible. And when we speak of hermeneutics, we tend to move quickly to methods and steps to getting biblical interpretation right. Bonhoeffer was interested in such things. He spent a great deal of time learning how to exegete the text, and he made sure his students learned such skills as well. But he was also deeply concerned about our *approach* to Scripture, our "posture"

[26] Cited in Bethge, *Dietrich Bonhoeffer*, 442.
[27] *DBWE* 13:322.
[28] *DBWE* 13:322.
[29] *DBWE* 13:323.
[30] *DBWE* 13:323.

before Scripture. For Bonhoeffer, how we read the Bible is far more about our approach to the Bible than about following a method to get the right interpretation. His approach to reading the Bible may be summed up in these five ways:

1. We read the Bible directly—it is God's Word *to us*.
2. We read the Bible prayerfully and meditatively.
3. We read the Bible collectively.
4. We read the Bible submissively.
5. We read the Bible obediently.

Let's look at each of these.

We Read the Bible Directly

We start with the Bible as God's Word to us directly. In a passage from *Life Together*, we see what this means:

> We become a part of what once took place for our salvation. Forgetting and losing ourselves, we, too, pass through the Red Sea, through the desert, across the Jordan into the promised land. With Israel we fall into doubt and unbelief and through punishment and repentance experience again God's help and faithfulness.[31]

We are not mere spectators of biblical history. Rather, "we are torn out of our own existence and set down in the midst of the holy history of God on earth."[32] And it is only in Scripture that we come to know our own history.[33]

We can all too easily approach Scripture the way a scientist approaches a specimen on the dissecting table, impassionate and disconnected from the object. Bonhoeffer reminds us that God's Word is no such object and that we are not scientists. We belong to God and he has given us, addressed directly to us, his Word. As Inge (Karding) Sembritzki, one of Bonhoeffer's students at Berlin, remembers, "[Bonhoeffer] taught us that we had to read the Bible as it was directed at us, as the Word of God directly to us." She adds, "He repeated this to us very early on, that the whole thing comes from that."[34] By the "whole thing" she was talking about the Christian life, life

---

[31] *LT*, 53.
[32] *LT*, 53.
[33] *LT*, 54.
[34] Inge (Karding) Sembritzki, cited in Eric Metaxas, *Bonhoeffer: Pastor, Martyr, Prophet, Spy* (Nashville: Thomas Nelson, 2010), 128–29.

in the church, and theology—everything springs from reading the Bible as God's Word directly to us.

We Read the Bible Prayerfully and Meditatively

Of life at Finkenwalde, Bonhoeffer writes, "We have learnt here once again to read the Bible prayerfully." He goes on to describe the details, starting with the morning and evening devotions "in which we hear the word of the Bible continuously":

> After we have read a Psalm together, each of the brethren in turn reads one passage from the Old Testament and one from the New, interspersed with verses from hymns and leading up to a free prayer and the Our Father said together. In the daily period for meditation we consider a fairly short biblical text appointed for the whole week.[35]

These practices described are over and above the course instruction at the seminary. Bonhoeffer instituted both a daily public reading of large portions of Scripture and a daily time of private meditation. In those public readings, the seminary community worked through the Bible, always including a chapter from the Psalms. This practice of *lectio continua*, Bonhoeffer explains in *Life Together*, is necessary because the Bible is a corpus, a whole.[36] But when it came to the meditation times of the day, Bonhoeffer preferred a different approach. Here he selected a short text for the whole week. Putting these two practices together, students were getting the view of both the forest and the trees.

The stress was on meditation on these short texts. Students weren't to use the time for sermon writing or for working the passage into their course papers. They were to allow the text to take deep root in their lives. They returned to the same text each day for a week, turning the text over and over and over again. Many of the students bucked this practice of forced meditation, especially those who transferred from other seminaries and universities. It was foreign to them and they reacted against it. But soon they were won over.

Bonhoeffer modeled such reading himself. He loved books and counted them among his most precious possessions. But the book he regarded the highest was his brother Walter's Bible. Walter Bonhoeffer was wounded in

---

[35] Bonhoeffer, "A Greeting from the Finkenwalde Seminary," in Robertson, *The Way to Freedom*, 35.
[36] *LT*, 53.

France, fighting along the front during the First World War. He died five days later in a field hospital on April 28, 1918. At Bonhoeffer's confirmation in 1921, his mother, Paula, gave him the Bible that had belonged to Walter. Dietrich kept that Bible for the rest of his life and used it for his daily time of prayerful and meditative reading.

We Read the Bible Collectively

That Bonhoeffer advocated the reading of the Bible collectively is obvious enough by now. But this means far more than reading it aloud together or in community. As we saw above in chapter 2, Bonhoeffer lists seven ministries, among them the ministry of proclaiming. You might recall that Bonhoeffer claimed the ministry of the Word to be "the ultimate and highest service [that] can . . . be rendered."[37] When he tells us to read the Bible collectively, he's actually telling us that we proclaim the Bible to each other, and that's the best thing we can do for each other. We speak the word to each other, from one life to another life.

This speaking, Bonhoeffer observes, "is beset with infinite perils."[38] People can use the Word like a weapon, cutting others down. People can use the Word to gain power over others. People manipulate the Word in the sole service of manipulating others. But those are only the bad intentions. Even with good intentions we can walk into the high grass. Nevertheless, we have a duty to speak the Word to each other. Our temptation is to speak from our preference and our own sense of things when we challenge each other. Or maybe we never get beyond playful talk with one another. But we have to "declare God's Word and will to one another."[39] We do this knowing that we are sinners, too, "lonely and lost" without help. So Bonhoeffer encourages us: "We speak to one another on the basis of the help we both need. We admonish each other to go the way Christ bids us to go. We warn one another against the disobedience that is our common destruction."[40] Reading the Bible collectively means we are bound together by, through, and in the Word of God.

We Read the Bible Submissively

We may not like what we read in the Bible. We may not always be able to make sense of what we read. We may not think that what we are reading

---

[37] *LT*, 103.
[38] *LT*, 104.
[39] *LT*, 105.
[40] *LT*, 106.

is even sensible at all. But Scripture does not rest with us; it rests with God who gave it. Bonhoeffer put it boldly: "The Word of God *rules*."[41] Our role is to serve, to submit. The Word's role is to rule. Returning to the Bethel Confession, we find these words: "We are not the judges of God's Word in the Bible; instead, the Bible is given to us so that through it we may submit ourselves to Christ's judgment."[42]

Theological liberalism errs fundamentally when it submits the Word of God to its own preferences and dictates. The rationalism of modernity sets up the human mind as the ultimate authority in epistemology (matters of knowledge and truth). If something accords with our notion of reason, then it counts for truth. In *Ethics*, Bonhoeffer will call this the "cult of the ratio."[43] This basic principle forms the bedrock conviction of higher criticism. Miracles do not accord with reason. They are *not rational* explanations. Therefore they are irrational. Consequently, we should rethink whether or not they are genuine historical events, and whether they are authentically recorded in Scripture. Maybe they are the figment of overexcited imaginations. And so on it goes. The issue here is one of posture. The Word of God is either over us or under us. Either we submit to it or we force it to submit to us.

What theological conservatives need to guard against, though, is thinking that because we affirm the Bible to be God's inerrant and authoritative word, we have therefore submitted to the Bible. We can be conservatively confessional and functionally liberal. In other words, submitting to the Bible is far more than affirming an orthodox statement of Scripture. Affirming such a statement is crucial and essential. We should never minimize that. But affirming a high view of Scripture is only the first step of submission. We fully submit to God's Word when we accept its authority over our lives as we read it.

Submitting to Scripture is a sort of halfway house between reading the Bible and obeying it. If we want to see God's Word at work in our lives, submission is the posture we must adopt.

We Read the Bible Obediently

Finally, we read the Bible obediently. In one of his London sermons, Bonhoeffer references how we like to add "ornamentation" to things. We plant

---

[41] *DBWE* 16:495, emphasis his.
[42] *DBWE* 12:376.
[43] *DBWE* 6:115.

flower beds. We hang pictures on walls. Artists embellish landscapes; they don't merely copy what they see. We look at the beauty present in the natural world, and we feel the urge to add to it, to decorate it. Bonhoeffer explains, though, that "the Word of God needs no ornamentation," for "it is clothed in its own beauty, its own glory."[44] But then he backpedals, noting there is one thing that those who love God's Word can bring forth to decorate and adorn it: "Those who have loved this Word of God throughout two thousand years have not let themselves be prevented from bringing the finest they had with which to adorn it. And what could be the finest if not that which is unseen, namely, an obedient heart?"[45]

In one of the London sermons, Bonhoeffer quips that we have made "the church into a playground for all sorts of feelings of ours, instead of a place where God's word is obediently received and believed. . . . We keep thinking we have God in our power instead of allowing God to have power over us."[46] He continues, God is "demanding that we hand ourselves over, in life and death, in heart and soul and body."[47] This kind of obedience comes rarely. Maybe that is why we neglect to read God's Word. We know all too well that it requires things of us. The Bible puts obligations smack down upon our comfortable and self-sure lives.

As Bonhoeffer was preaching this—and thinking about unmitigated obedience to the Word as a necessary corollary to belief in the Bible as the true, divine revelation—he was reading the Sermon on the Mount (meditating actually) and beginning the early stages of writing *The Cost of Discipleship.* He waded into those waters carefully because he knew he really hadn't read the Bible—any text in the Bible—until he submitted in obedience to it.

Conclusion: When All You Have Is the Word

Martin Luther once said, "We can spare everything except the Word."[48] In the context, he was speaking of the church. But the same is true of our Christian life. In the Word we find the gospel. In the Word we find comfort. In the Word we find challenge. In the Word we find the Word, the incarnate Logos. We find Christ and his call upon our lives.

---

[44] *DBWE* 13:355.
[45] *DBWE* 13:355.
[46] *DBWE* 13:323–24.
[47] *DBWE* 13:324.
[48] Martin Luther, *Luther's Works,* vol. 53, *Liturgy and Hymns,* ed. Ulrich S. Leupold (Philadelphia: Fortress, 1965), 14.

Many of Bonhoeffer's prison letters to his family and friends speak of how he was bearing up. He knew of their anxieties for him, so he offered them assurances of his well-being. When he did so, he usually referenced reading. He read all sorts of books, whatever friends and family could smuggle in to him. But the book he returned to again and again was the Bible. He liked to tell his family and friends what he was reading in the Bible. In a letter to Bethge, he shares, "I am reading the Bible straight through from cover to cover, and have just got as far as Job, which I am particularly fond of. I read the Psalms every day, as I have done for years; I know them and love them more than any other book."[49] He was in prison. The world was at war. Hitler was in command. In 1943, when Bonhoeffer wrote this particular letter, there was no end in sight to any of these three facts. But Bonhoeffer had his Bible, he had Job, and he had the Psalms.

This practice of reading the Bible was no "prison conversion" for Bonhoeffer. He didn't turn to the Bible because he had nothing else to do at Tegel. We see this in a letter to his brother-in-law Rüdiger Schleicher. Schleicher was theologically liberal, and Bonhoeffer wrote to him to stake out how different his own position was from that of his brother-in-law. At the end of the letter he describes how it has been for himself since he has submitted to the Bible as the Word of God over him: "I read it in the morning and in the evening, often during the day as well, and every day I consider a text which I have chosen for the whole week, and try to sink deeply into it, so as really to hear what it is saying. I know that without this I could not live properly any longer."[50] When it comes to living the Christian life, we can spare everything except the Word.

When it comes to the church, we also can spare everything except the Word. In a London sermon, Bonhoeffer said, "We talk too much about false, trivial human things and ideas in the church and too little about God. . . . We make the church into a playground for all sorts of feelings of ours, instead of a place where God's Word is obediently received and believed."[51]

In our lives and in our churches, we can spare everything but the prayerful and meditative reading of the Word, the attentive listening to the preaching of it, and the submissive obeying of its demands on our lives. Bonhoeffer knew that he couldn't live without it.

---

[49] Bonhoeffer to his parents, May 15, 1943, *LPP*, 40.
[50] Cited in Metaxas, *Bonhoeffer*, 137.
[51] Dietrich Bonhoeffer, "Ambassadors for Christ," in *The Collected Sermons of Dietrich Bonhoeffer*, ed. Isabel Best (Minneapolis: Fortress, 2012), 91. I am indebted to Ryan Diehl for drawing my attention to this quote.

CHAPTER 5

PRAYER

Luther said that as a shoemaker makes shoes and a tailor clothes, so also must a Christian pray. . . . Prayer is the heart of Christian life.

DIETRICH BONHOEFFER, 1930

Brother, till the night be past, Pray for me!

DIETRICH BONHOEFFER,
"NIGHT VOICES IN TEGEL," 1944

John Calvin once likened prayer to a treasure chest buried in one's backyard. Imagine knowing there is such a treasure chest, right at our disposal, and never bothering to dig it up. That's exactly what happens when we fail to pray.[1]

From the beginning of his pastoral ministry and theological work, Bonhoeffer stressed the necessity of prayer. We see this in some of his early preaching, such as his sermon on 1 Thessalonians 5:16–18 given on July 12, 1930. In Christ, God's will consists of three things: joyfulness, prayer, and gratitude. "Prayer is the heart of the Christian life," he tells the congregation.[2] In his first dissertation, from 1927, he commends intercessory prayer as the hallmark of the church. To prove his point, he cites Russian

---

[1] John Calvin, *Truth for All Time: Brief Outline of the Christian Faith*, trans. Stuart Olyott (Edinburgh: Banner of Truth, 1998); 88; originally written in 1537.
[2] *DBWE* 10:577.

theologian Alexei Khomiakov's observation, "The blood of the church is prayer for each other."[3] To round it off, we have his personal reflections from his diary. In an entry from 1929, he recalls, "Congregational prayer sent shivers down my spine."[4] This salient memory leads him to state, "Where a people prays, there is the church."[5]

Right from the very outset, Bonhoeffer stressed the necessity of prayer. And at the end of his life's journey, prayer sustained him. On November 29, 1943, the day after the first Sunday in Advent that year, Bonhoeffer wrote to his friend Bethge:

> Now there's something I must tell you personally: the heavy air raids, especially the last one, when the windows of the sick bay were blown out by the landmine, and bottles and medical supplies fell down from the cupboards and shelves, and I lay on the floor in the darkness with little hope of coming through the attack safely, led me back quite simply to prayer and the Bible.[6]

Too often and far too tragically, we take prayer as a luxury, thinking—but never saying—that while prayer is nice and important, we might just be able to get along without it. Bonhoeffer, from the beginning, knew such misguided thoughts on prayer take us down dangerous roads. By no means a luxury, prayer is a necessity. Prayer is necessary for the Christian life and necessary for our life together in the church.

Because Bonhoeffer thought so highly of prayer, he offers much on the subject throughout his life and his writings. When he formed Finkenwalde, the seminary to serve the Confessing Church, he made it a priority to teach students how to pray. In fact, for him, the two most essential ingredients for pastoral ministry were learning and knowing how to pray and learning and knowing how to read the Bible. In addition to prayer and pastoral ministry, Bonhoeffer also has much to say about praying alone in private devotions and praying together. He offers sermons on prayer, writes of the Lord's prayer and the Christian life in *The Cost of Discipleship*, and writes of prayer's necessity in many of his letters. Finally, in addition to all of this talk about prayer, he prayed. He prayed a lot. Sometimes he wrestled, agonized really, over what he took to be his own ineffectualness at praying.

---

[3] Cited in *DBWE* 1:186.
[4] *DBWE* 10:58.
[5] *DBWE* 10:58.
[6] *LPP*, 149.

Sometimes he even revealed his doubts about the effectualness of prayer. But in the fog of those trying times and doubting moments, he found his way back to prayer.

We see him on the floors of Tegel Prison, bombs exploding, windows bursting, bottles and wares crashing to the floor. And we see him praying. He's praying because, as he learned from Luther, if shoemakers make shoes and tailors make clothes, then Christians pray.

Refuting "Blasphemous Ignorance": Prayer and the Pastoral Ministry

Soon after Bonhoeffer took charge of the Confessing Church's seminary, which met first at Zingst and then at Finkenwalde, criticism poured in. Actually, it might be better to say it swirled around. The criticisms did make their way to Bonhoeffer's own ears, but only after they had germinated and grown like weeds. By the time the criticism reached him, he was forced into damage control.

The essence of the criticism, which came even from some of the Zingst and Finkenwalde students themselves, seems to be that Bonhoeffer was turning the seminary into a monastery, complete with rigorous times of forced and lengthy private meditation and prayer. So committed to these practices was he that his critics also charged him and the seminary with legalism. As for the first charge, Bonhoeffer never meant such disciplines to substitute for rigorous ministerial education, the roll-up-your-sleeves kind of exegetical and theological—even philosophical—work that belongs in training up pastors. But Bonhoeffer realized something. His students did not know how to pray. Without prayer, their pastoral ministries would run shallow, no matter how quickly and eloquently they could run their exegetical circles. As for the charge of legalism, he simply averred that prayer is a duty and that duty requires discipline. These young seminarians were *in training*. Without discipline, they likely wouldn't learn their Greek verb paradigms either. So he forced them to pray.

Bonhoeffer defended himself against the criticisms and commended his approach in a letter to Karl Barth. Barth had heard of some of Bonhoeffer's practices and had his own doubts as to their effectiveness. Bonhoeffer's letter clears the air. He recalls his time as a theological student at Berlin, remembering that no one taught him to pray there. He also points out that even in the Confessing Church the need to teach pastors how to pray "has not been met."[7] He's incredulous that some would think him legalistic for teaching and requiring his students to pray. To counter this charge of legalism, he contends, "How can it possibly be legalistic for a Christian to learn what prayer is, and to spend a fair amount of time learning it?"[8] Bonhoeffer then references one of his critics, a leading figure in the Confessing Church, who told him, "We haven't such time for meditation now; the ordinands must learn to preach and to catechize." Bonhoeffer tells Barth what he thinks: "This either shows a total lack of understanding of young theologians today, or else a blasphemous ignorance of how preaching and teaching come about."[9]

Preaching and teaching, the public and platform aspects of ministry, come about only on the basis of prayer and Bible reading and meditation, the more private and personal aspects of ministry. Reflecting on this, Bonhoeffer scholar Geffrey Kelly reveals Bonhoeffer's sense of the purpose of seminary: "The seminary was to become not just a protracted series of lessons on how to preach and catechize, but an occasion for ordinands to steep themselves in prayer and meditation in order themselves to become bearers of God's Word, the absolute precondition for being a good preacher or teacher."[10]

Pastors need, like everyone else, to pray for themselves and for others. Bonhoeffer once referred to the church as a fellowship of sinners. That's why forgiveness is such a significant part of the Lord's Prayer. Because we are sinners we must pray for ourselves. Our leaders and pastors are no exception here. We sometimes think of them as superheroes, possessing extraordinary spiritual strength. But they don't possess it. The day they begin to think they do can be circled on the calendar. A bad outcome will surely follow that date. Pastors must pray for themselves. But Bonhoeffer also puts a heavy burden on pastors to pray for others.

Intercessory prayer functions significantly in Bonhoeffer's thought and theology. This should come as no surprise. Given his sense of how closely knit we are to one another in community through our union with Christ, we must pray for one another. Of course, all Christians must intercede in prayer for one another. Bonhoeffer's thoughts and directives on this will be looked at later in this chapter. But there is a special intercession between pastor and congregation, an intercession that serves as a two-way street.

---

[7] Bonhoeffer to Karl Barth, September 19, 1936, cited in Eberhard Bethge, *Dietrich Bonhoeffer: A Biography*, enl. ed. (Minneapolis: Fortress, 2000), 464.

[8] Ibid., 465.

[9] Ibid., 464–65.

[10] Geffrey B. Kelly, "Editor's Introduction," *DBWE* 10:147.

"A congregation that does not pray for the ministry of its pastor," Bonhoeffer warns, "is no longer a congregation."[11] He then adds, "A pastor who does not pray daily for his congregation is no longer a pastor."[12]

Bill Hybels expressed it about as well as you can in his book title *Too Busy Not to Pray*. Of course, our tendency is to drop out the "Not." We vainly think we are too busy to pray, and we foolishly go about our business without prayer. Neglecting prayer is even more of a temptation for people who are busy for Christ and busy in doing kingdom work. This dynamic explains why Bonhoeffer stressed teaching about prayer and requiring would-be pastors in seminary to pray. There's no pastoral ministry without it. There's no Christian life without it.

How Not to Pray

Not only do *pastors* need to be taught how to pray. We *all* need to be taught how to seek God in prayer. One of the reasons is that we often pray wrongly. My uncle, Chuck Nichols, a seminary professor and minister in Canada, tells the story of a particular professor he had while back in college. This professor had a reputation for precision—theological precision, grammatical precision, precision in pretty much everything. He also took it upon himself to correct people—students especially, but also visiting chapel speakers, people on the street, pretty much anyone. That was his reputation.

This college professor had students successively open the class in prayer. Given his reputation, they dreaded doing so. As soon as they would finish, he would begin his litany of errors in their prayers. When he asked my uncle to pray, my uncle simply refused—well, not so simply, as refusing this professor was something rarely ventured. But my uncle had a reason for his refusal: "When I pray, sir, I pray to God, not to you."

When we talk about praying wrongly, we tend to think of praying wrongly *theologically*. This is what so concerned the professor. But that's not exactly what Bonhoeffer has in mind. It's true that we can be theologically imprecise in our praying; we can even be theologically wrong in our praying. That's why Bonhoeffer commended the Lord's Prayer not simply as a model for prayer, but as the prayer we should pray. We learn to pray theologically well when we have the Lord's Prayer as part of our mental and spiritual furniture and framework.

[11] *DBWE* 13:325.
[12] *DBWE* 13:325.

But praying wrongly *theologically* is not what concerns Bonhoeffer the most. The kind of wrong praying that deeply concerns him is prayer about the "I" when it should be about the "You." In this case, the You is none other than God. The Pharisee publicly demonstrated his praying self in public like a peacock on parade. That's praying wrongly. Bonhoeffer adds that such praying doesn't always have to happen in public. It can also happen in private. When we make prayer only about ourselves—about our agenda—we pray wrongly. Bonhoeffer comments, "I listen to myself; I hear myself."[13]

Bonhoeffer does not mean we never pray for our needs. He's concerned about the order of our petitions. More importantly, he's concerned about the purpose that lies behind our petitions. For Bonhoeffer, prayer means far more than simply offering up a list of petitions. He stops us in our tracks, forcing us to deal with what prayer fundamentally means and accomplishes. Prayer means bending our desires to God's determinations, bringing our petitions in line with his priorities, and having his kingdom and not our agenda at the center. Simply put, prayer is the "orientation of one's life to God."[14]

In this sense, prayer is not unlike salvation. Taking a page from Luther's playbook, Bonhoeffer understands prayer to be like salvation: in both instances we need to stop looking within ourselves, stop being driven by the self, and stop aiming for self-achievement and self-betterment. Prayer starts and ends with God. Praying rightly disciplines us to move our orientation away from self and toward God.

The christology at the center of Bonhoeffer's theology is also very much present and accounted for in his thoughts on prayer. Commenting on Paul's command to "pray without ceasing" (1 Thess. 5:17), Bonhoeffer exhorts all who will hear, "Let your entire life be a prayer, let it be turned to God and be a response to God's word in Christ."[15] Bonhoeffer adds, "In Christ, our prayer has its foundation."[16] Christ is the ground and basis for prayer, Christ enables us to pray, and Christ even teaches us to pray.

How to Pray

Like a good Lutheran, Bonhoeffer used the Lord's Prayer. Luther saw training up the next generation in the church as his main task. He embarked

---

[13] *DBWE* 4:154.
[14] *DBWE* 10:573.
[15] *DBWE* 10:577.
[16] *DBWE* 10:577.

on writing a catechism, structuring it around the Apostles' Creed, the Ten Commandments, and the Lord's Prayer, a perfect curriculum for doctrine, ethics, and living the Christian life. Ministers in the Lutheran Church work through these texts and Luther's Catechism with their young charges, preparing them for their confirmation. This is what Bonhoeffer did, too. In Barcelona, in Berlin, and in London he gently took children by the hand and led them through the Lord's Prayer. Bonhoeffer also continues to lead us in understanding and valuing the practice of prayer in the writings he's left behind.

Early in his academic career at Berlin, Bonhoeffer took on the extra task of leading some rather unruly boys through Luther's Catechism for their confirmation. This was at Zion's Church in the Prenzlauer Berg district of Berlin—the other side of the tracks from Bonhoeffer's upbringing. This particular group of confirmands had driven away their other teachers. No adults in the church were keen on stepping in, and so the minister crossed his fingers as he pinned the request to the board at the University of Berlin, hoping to get a student in need of some experience at church work. In walked Bonhoeffer, the professor. Unintimidated by these boys, Bonhoeffer set right to work. One of these boys many years later saw an advertisement for a conference on Dietrich Bonhoeffer sponsored by the International Bonhoeffer Society. He boarded a train in Berlin, the city he never left. Over the decades, this man had seen the city reduced to rubble, then rebuilt. He had seen a wall go up, and then a wall go down. And over those decades he had never forgotten the almost magical moments a young theology professor from the university shared with him and his mates. This man, who hardly ever ventured beyond Berlin, made the eighty-five-kilometer trip to the conference and told the scholars gathered to read and discuss papers that he was one of Bonhoeffer's confirmands from Zion's Church fifty-three years prior. He wanted someone to know how much Bonhoeffer meant to him. Such was his gratitude for what Bonhoeffer had taught him and done for him.

At the center of that teaching was prayer. Bonhoeffer divided the Lord's Prayer into the "You petitions" and the "our petitions." The "You petitions" concern God:

Hallowed be thy name.
Thy kingdom come,
Thy will be done in earth, as it is in heaven.

The "our petitions" relate to us:

> Give us this day our daily bread.
> And forgive us our debts, as we forgive our debtors.
> And lead us not into temptation, but deliver us from evil.
>   (Matt. 6:9–13, KJV)

Reflecting on the first three petitions of the Lord's Supper, the You petitions, Bonhoeffer states, "This is very important, Jesus tells us that when you want to pray to God, think first of all about God."[17] He adds, "Leave yourselves completely aside for a moment and see how much more important it is that we first learn to say: your name, your kingdom, your will. First you, and again you."[18] As mentioned above, prayer is about God first; then it is about us. It's wrong to think and pray otherwise.

But once we have God firmly at the beginning, end, and center of our prayers, we bring our desires, needs, and petitions to him. Bonhoeffer notes how the "our petitions" concern both body and soul. He also observes, "We see now that when Jesus has us ask for the forgiveness of our sin immediately after asking for our daily bread, he must have meant that this forgiveness represents something that is especially necessary for our soul, indeed as necessary as bread is for our body."[19] Without bread we die. Without forgiveness, the dead soul stays dead. There is no spiritual life without forgiveness.

In the course of unpacking this petition, Bonhoeffer looks at forgiveness as both a disposition and an action. We are forgiven, removed from the punishment of God's wrath through the work of Christ. Bonhoeffer speaks of the "two frightening words" of "God's anger and God's punishment" standing over us.[20] In our sinful state we have "a relationship of debt" to God. In Christ, we are forgiven, the debt now removed and the relationship gloriously transformed from debt to sonship. Forgiveness is a disposition.

But forgiveness is also an action or actions, as forgiven people need forgiveness. So we request it of God. Bonhoeffer explains, "God wants only that we bring our sin before him; then God will forgive us."[21] And he does this "from pure love."[22] This forgiveness, though, comes with an obligation:

---

[17] *DBWE* 10:560.
[18] *DBWE* 10:560.
[19] *DBWE* 10:561.
[20] *DBWE* 10:564.
[21] *DBWE* 10:568.
[22] *DBWE* 10:568.

to forgive others. Bonhoeffer shows the connection here: "Now, if instead of anger and punishment a person experiences but love from God, that person will have but one great wish. What is that wish? To share that love."[23] We share that love by forgiving others. These are the things Bonhoeffer taught this unruly bunch from one of Berlin's roughest neighborhoods. And he managed to get them ready. When the Sunday came for their confirmation and first Communion, they were all dressed in new suits—suits Bonhoeffer had paid for himself.

Years later, Bonhoeffer wrote on the Lord's Prayer in his classic text *The Cost of Discipleship*. There he says that the Lord's Prayer is not just a general model for prayer but, "rather, it is what should be prayed."[24] This prayer leads us into complete clarity and certainty in our praying. Bonhoeffer also reminds us of how this prayer starts with the words, "Our Father." This is "the request of the child to the heart of the father."[25] And he reminds us: "In Jesus we have come to know the kindliness of the Father. In the name of the Son of God we may call God our Father."[26]

In *Discipleship*, as in his confirmation class, Bonhoeffer stresses the necessity of forgiving others. As Christians, we "live in the fellowship of other sinners."[27] Only forgiveness makes such living with other sinners possible.

Bonhoeffer has more to say about prayer than his comments on the Lord's Prayer. He sees prayer as a crucial discipline to be practiced both alone and together. For each category of praying, he offers both sound instruction and a solid example.

Praying Alone

In terms of our praying alone, Bonhoeffer starts with the discipline of praying Scripture. This hearkens back to our discussion about praying wrongly. By praying Scripture, we are adjusting ourselves, transforming ourselves, refashioning ourselves. We are naturally calibrated to turn inward, to pervert God's direction. God's Word is the healthiest corrective for our wrong orientation.

Praying Scripture is actually stillness and silence before Scripture. In *Life Together*, Bonhoeffer speaks of his own time as "days when talkative-

[23] *DBWE* 10:569.
[24] *DBWE* 4:155.
[25] *DBWE* 4:153.
[26] *DBWE* 4:155.
[27] *DBWE* 4:158.

ness prevails."[28] We like to talk, but we must listen—not only to others (as we have seen) but to God in Scripture. Bonhoeffer explains, "Silence before the Word leads to right hearing and thus also to right speaking of the Word of God at the right time."[29] Silence also means, for Bonhoeffer, meditation. He offers a rather strict understanding of meditation. This is no occasion, he intones, "for spiritual experiments."[30] This is not some Buddhist-style meditation that lets the mind wander off into some fictional Never Never Land. He absolutely links meditation to the content of the Word, "the solid ground."[31] If we do not have a Scripture-saturated approach to our praying, we risk becoming "victims of our own emptiness."[32]

Bonhoeffer explains how praying Scripture works itself out in our daily walk: "According to a word of Scripture we pray for clarification for our day, for preservation from sin, for growth in sanctification, for faithfulness and strength in our work."[33] Bonhoeffer then adds these most encouraging words: "Because God's word has found its fulfillment in Jesus Christ, all prayers that we pray conforming to this word are certainly heard and answered in Jesus Christ."[34]

Of course when it comes to praying Scripture, Bonhoeffer was drawn to the Psalms, "one book that differs from all other books in the Bible in that it contains only prayers."[35] This line comes from the introduction to his *Prayerbook of the Bible: An Introduction to the Psalms*, published in 1940. Here we especially see Bonhoeffer's christology again. As chapter 2 presented the case for christology at the center of Bonhoeffer's theology, here we see christology at the center of Bonhoeffer's thoughts on prayer. We tend to come to the Psalms and ask what they have to do with us. Bonhoeffer thinks that's starting with the wrong question. "We must not," he writes, "first ask what they have to do with us, but what they have to do with Jesus Christ."[36] The Psalms point to and find their center in Christ. Through our union with Christ, we enter into the Psalms. They become ours.

This "great school of prayer," the Psalter, offers us prayers on creation and God's goodness to us, the history of God's work of redemption, the

[28] *LT*, 79.
[29] *LT*, 79.
[30] *LT*, 81.
[31] *LT*, 81.
[32] *LT*, 84.
[33] *LT*, 85.
[34] *LT*, 85.
[35] *DBWE* 5:156.
[36] *DBWE* 5:157.

coming of the Messiah, the church and the people of God, life and work (by which Bonhoeffer means the meaning of life and issues of fulfillment and happiness in life), suffering, guilt, enemies and oppressors, death, the resurrection, and the life to come. In short, the Psalms touch on everything. Quite simply, praying the Psalms helps us pray better.[37]

When we initially come to Christ, we likely have only a surface sense of our sin. We know it's heinous, we know it's a cosmic and eternal offense, and we know the cost of our sin. But being in Christ for a while and maturing in Christ are the normal prerequisites to truly seeing the depths of our sin. In Christ, we can truly plumb the depths of our need and our neediness. So we pray. We pray for ourselves and for our soul's most dire need: forgiveness. C. S. Lewis once wrote that true forgiveness means seeing sin "in all its horror, dirt, meanness, and malice, and nevertheless being wholly reconciled to the man who has done it. That, and only that, is forgiveness, and that we can always have from God if we ask for it."[38]

If we revisit Bonhoeffer's Berlin sermon on Paul's command to "pray without ceasing" (1 Thess. 5:17), we see that three things are essential to our Christian identity: joyfulness and rejoicing, praying, and gratitude. Bonhoeffer titles the sermon "Christian Life under the Good News." It seems like there is much talk these days about gospel-centered living. Bonhoeffer sees 1 Thessalonians 5:16–18 as the essence of gospel-centered living, life under the gospel. We rejoice *in Christ*; we pray without ceasing *in Christ*; and we live from a position of gratitude *in Christ*. Concerning prayer, Bonhoeffer laments that prayer was moved to the margins of Christian living in his day. He asks some soul-searching questions regarding our neglect of prayer owing ultimately to our lukewarm hearts. Then he asks, "How many of us suffer from this poverty of prayer and alienation from prayer?"[39] A sad description, "poverty of prayer" is all too true of many of us.

If we live in poverty of prayer, we certainly do not live well spiritually. Bonhoeffer explains why:

> Praying means to turn one's life to God and to his Word as revealed to us through Christ, to surrender, entrust our lives completely to God, to throw ourselves into God's arms, to grow together with God, to sense

---

[37] *DBWE* 5:177.
[38] C. S. Lewis, "On Forgiveness," in *The Weight of Glory and Other Addresses* (New York: HarperCollins, 1980), 181.
[39] *DBWE* 10:577.

God's life in our own lives. Praying means wanting to approach and to remain close to God because God has come close to us.[40]

Bonhoeffer preached this at twenty-five years of age. He knew something then that would stay with him the rest of his life. When imprisoned at Tegel he experienced, as can be imagined, dark and difficult days. On one such day he wrote down just how dismal he felt. He scratched out a series of words: dissatisfaction, tension, impatience, sick—profoundly alone. He even wrote, "suicide, not because of consciousness of guilt but because basically I am already dead."[41] Then at the bottom of this sheet are these words: "Overcoming *in prayer*."[42] Because God came close to us, we desire to approach him and stay close to God. And being close to God enables us to overcome. In Bonhoeffer's case, not at all unlike the psalmists, he overcame profound depths *in prayer*.

Praying Together: Intercession

Given everything we have learned and know about Bonhoeffer, we should certainly expect him to stress praying for others. In *Life Together*, he states: "A Christian fellowship lives and exists by intercession of its members for one another, or it collapses. I can no longer hate a brother for whom I pray, no matter how much trouble he causes me."[43] I have come to deeply appreciate Bonhoeffer's Christian realism in our evangelical culture of platitudes. He does not cherry coat the frustrations and conflicts in the Christian community.

The line "no matter how much trouble he causes me" reveals just how honest Bonhoeffer is when it comes to interpersonal conflict. He even admits what a "struggle" (using the German word *kampf*) it is to pray for someone who rubs us the wrong way. Bonhoeffer's own experience of such struggles ran the gamut from outright slander and calumny to those little irritants of others that come to the surface in close contact. In other words, Bonhoeffer experienced it all, from the struggles with real enemies who were out to get him (literally) to the struggles with young seminarians at Finkenwalde. The solution? Pray for them.

Bonhoeffer is not here using prayer as a means of manipulation, a tech-

---

[40] *DBWE* 5:577.
[41] Bonhoeffer, "Notes," May 8, 1943, *LPP*, 35.
[42] Ibid.
[43] *LT*, 86.

nique to trick our brains. In the course of intercessory prayer we learn of the depth of Christ's love for us and Christ's love for the other, even the erring brother or sister. Intercessory prayer for our brothers and sisters in Christ reminds us that they are persons "for whom Christ died."[44] Bonhoeffer continues: "Intercession means no more than to bring our brother into the presence of God, to see him under the cross of Jesus as a poor sinner in need of grace. Then everything in him that repels us falls away; we see him in all his destitution and need."[45] We owe intercession to God and to our brother, Bonhoeffer adds. Intercession is our obligation: "He who denies his neighbor the service of praying for him denies him the service of a Christian."[46]

Praying for each other also leads naturally to serving one another. Singer and songwriter Bruce Springsteen, at best a marginal Roman Catholic and by no means a professional theologian, sometimes has theologically acute things to say. In one of his songs he rasps in his New Jersey–bred voice, "With these hands, I pray Lord." Bonhoeffer would likely approve. In *Life Together*, he speaks of "intercessions for one another" that occur "without words."[47] We serve and "bear" one another as a natural extension of praying for one another. Prayer comes from our hearts and lips, but it also extends to our hands. As we have come to expect with Bonhoeffer, he advocates active praying, a praying with our hands. This is a pleasant blurring of the lines between the spiritual discipline of prayer and the action, with our hands, of service. Both are intercession.

Bonhoeffer was right to teach the young seminarians at Finkenwalde to pray. He was right when he stressed that his seminary would make prayer part and parcel of the experience. He was right when he saw that the height to which a pastoral ministry could go depended on the depth to which prayer had taken root. And he was right to see that the church's urgent task, in light of its urgent situation, is to pray. His own praying led to service and action, and his service and action came as a result of his praying.

Bonhoeffer once made the remarkable statement, "It has become all too clear that our age has little room at all for prayer."[48] It's remarkable in that it is both acutely right and acutely wrong at the same time. He was right: his age had neglected prayer. But his age wasn't the only one guilty of the charge. There are a variety of reasons we can offer up for such neglect of

---

[44] *LT*, 86.
[45] *LT*, 86.
[46] *LT*, 86–87.
[47] *LT*, 103.
[48] *DBWE* 10:576.

prayer. Not one of them, however, is valid. God has designed prayer as our lifeline. It is our means of communion with the triune God, the means by which our Savior, Creator, and Lord brings his will for our lives to fruition.

Conclusion: More Than Clocks

In June 1730, a handful of Cherokee Indian Chiefs crossed the Atlantic seeking an audience with King George II. They first appeared in court at Kensington Palace. They were there to sign treaties, to present their grievances against the French, and to petition the king for aid and support. They had to wait in the lobby for days, returning again and again until the king granted them an audience. They were finally granted their opportunity to present their petitions. Custom dictated that the king would signify his acceptance of their petition by giving them gifts. King George II gave the Cherokees clocks.

They were fine clocks, no doubt. Any English nobleman would be honored beyond words to have such a gift, and he would be just as sure to display the clocks prominently. But these Cherokee had no idea what these clocks were and had no use for them whatsoever. It's not even clear that they took the clocks home with them as they crossed the Atlantic on their return to the colonies. History is clearer on what became of the treaties King George II made with the Cherokee.

How opposite is prayer to the almighty God, sovereign King of the universe. We do not need to board a ship and travel thousands of miles and wait for days in a grand entrance hall. And when we do get an audience with this King, he does not give us clocks. He graciously grants to us exactly and precisely what we need. And we know that his promises are sure. He does not break treaties.

Bonhoeffer reminds us that the journey of prayer is actually far more costly than a transatlantic trip. Our journey of prayer into the presence of God cost the precious blood of Christ, God's Son. Christ's sacrifice grants us entrance to the Father's court. Christ's sacrifice grants us the good favor of receiving the King's gifts: the gift of participating in his kingdom, the gift of seeing God's will come to pass, the gift of forgiveness of sins, the gift of protection from temptation, the gift of deliverance from evil, and even the gift of daily bread. And Christ's sacrifice guarantees that all God's promises come true. Why would we want to be a people or a church or an age characterized by neglecting such great gifts?

CHAPTER 6

CONFESSION

I think I am right in saying that I would only achieve true inner clarity and honesty by really starting to take the Sermon on the Mount seriously.

DIETRICH BONHOEFFER, 1945

A young theological student should know that to pursue theology is to serve the true church of Christ, which is unwavering in confessing its Lord, and should live with this responsibility.

DIETRICH BONHOEFFER, 1933

For some reason theology often gets pitted against spirituality. We see this tension in such popular sayings as "I don't want to know *about* God. I want to know God." Think about telling your wife or husband that you don't want to know things about her or him; you only want to know her or him. That would not serve you very well. It makes no more sense to say it of God.

This tension between spirituality and theology leads to near-fatal consequences. When the church, either the local church or broader movements and associations, forges ahead with little attention to theology, it lives on borrowed time. The same is true for individual Christians. When careful theological reflection ranks low, you can almost start the watch and time the inevitable drift away from sound teaching and the true gospel.

Consider the idea of "knowing God" over "knowing about God." On the one hand, we can appreciate the underlying desire. God is not some object for our study, like something we would look up in an encyclopedia. We know God in relationship, in the full-orbed context of his covenant faithfulness to his redeemed people. But without knowing *about* God, we really don't know God at all. God has revealed himself to us, showing both his person and his character. He invites us in to learn about him. Frankly, it is impossible to know God without knowing about God. It is also dangerous, as we can quickly move away from his revelation of himself as the basis and content of our relationship with him and onto our own preconceptions and personal sensibilities of who God is and how he should act. Danger lurks in saying, "I don't want to know about God." We know God in knowing about God—that's a far better way to put it.

We seem especially susceptible to this pitting of spirituality against theology in American evangelical contexts. Perhaps we can chalk this up to the influence of pietism, which courses through the veins of many evangelicals. Pietism should not be confused with piety. Piety means simply the spiritual practices of praying, Bible reading and meditation, fasting, and gifts of charity. Piety means pious acts before God for others out of gratitude and love. Piety means trying to live a holy life. We should all practice piety and seek to live piously—that is, by the grace of God, through our union with Christ, and by the equipping and enabling of the Holy Spirit. Piety is a good thing. Pietism, however, means something altogether different.

Pietism reduces Christianity to personal acts of holiness. It also tends toward emotionalism. Pietism stresses personal striving after God. It cares little for theological reflection. In pietism one typically hears of orthodoxy only when the topic is "dead orthodoxy." What sends pietism off the rails is its reductionism. It's one thing to stress holy living. It's quite another to stress holy living in a way that excludes biblical fidelity and orthodox theology. Pietism errs because it rejects the need to have *both* right living *and* right theology.

Pietism actually began in Germany among the work of Lutheran churchmen Phillip Jakob Spener and August Hermann Francke. Spener's 1675 work *Pia desideria* (*Heart's Desire*) marks the birth of and gives shape to pietism. From Germany, pietism migrated to England, having a significant impact on John Wesley and early Methodism. This early Methodism brought pietism to America from the 1790s through the 1820s. Various German and Swiss immigrants, facing persecution in their homelands, took pietism with them throughout the eighteenth century. These different streams all converged, resulting in pietism's firm entrenchment in American Christianity. It would be safe to say that by the nineteenth century, pietism had long since dislodged Puritanism as the dominant force in American religious life.

We need to understand that pietism is problematic not because it stresses the pursuit of holiness or because of its emphasis on serving others and on works of charity. Pietism is problematic because of what it leaves out. It tends to leave out theological confession and careful reflection and analytical argument. And, as it tends to be self-focused, it leaves out the focus on the grace of God. It does not stress nearly enough the work of the triune God in our lives. Rather, pietism stresses our striving to be holy in our own strength and by our own devices. Though giving lip service to grace, pietism functionally becomes about our own efforts, our own kicking and striving and clawing our way to spirituality and holiness.

I have seen pietism in many shapes and sizes. I have seen it at youth rallies and camps when Christianity is reduced to being "really, really passionate about God." I have seen it in revival settings where the focus is on one's emotional encounter and emotional expression. I have heard it or read it expressed by those who believe that thinking too much or too deeply is actually an enemy of Christianity. I have seen it in those who reduce Christianity to the mantra of the little engine, "I think I can, I think I can, I think I can," as they strive to pull the train up the hill. We could haul out statistics and Gallup polls to prove the point, or we could simply tour American evangelicalism and all too readily see pietism.

Pietism and the hold it has on American evangelicals bears much responsibility for this regrettable tension between matters of the spiritual life and matters of theology. But what about theologians? Do they bear any of the responsibility for this tension? Maybe they do. We will see this shortly, but Bonhoeffer sounds the note clearly and loudly: theologians serve the church. Theologians do not serve the academy, nor do they serve each other. Theologians serve the church. When theologians neglect to see their primary calling as serving the church, they often spin out a theology of little relevance to church life and to churchgoers, causing those churchgoers to run *from* theology and not *to* it.

This tendency is dangerous on two counts. First, such a theology that serves the academy and fellow professional theologians risks stopping at knowing *about* God, while never getting around to knowing God. Second, such theology creates systems and even an entire vocabulary that sound foreign to laity.

Some further explanation is in order here. Theologians have well served the church by their academic work. Even the language—as foreign sounding as it may be—is helpful. Take the word *Trinity*, for instance. This theological construct, a gift from the church father Tertullian, offers a most helpful way to express the wide and complex teaching of Scripture on the nature and being of God. The rather sophisticated theological debates over the nature of person and substance, as the church fathers wrestled with the biblical texts and challenges to them, have been most beneficial, even essential, to the church's life and practice in the centuries since. But when the work of theologians becomes so dense and so abstract that it extends far beyond the reach of the laity, the result will be that the laity will run in the opposite direction safe into the arms of experience and vague "spirituality." The trappings of pietism look far more inviting than the obfuscations of theologians. Let the reader understand: the work of theologians is good and necessary, but at some points a line can be crossed, with the reverse effect of turning people off to healthy and edifying theological reflection. Pietism is a culprit in this tragic tension between spirituality and theology. But theologians can be culpable, too. Sadly, there's enough blame to go around.

Bonhoeffer confronted pietism in his day. He also confronted the opposite of pietism, rationalism. If pietism is about the emotions, rationalism concerns the intellect. There is a difference between being rational or using rationality and rational*ism*, just like the difference between piety and piet*ism*. To be rational is a good thing. God created us as intellectual beings. He gave us minds to develop. God intends us to use our minds in the exploration of his world and of his Word. But that's not rationalism. Rationalism disdains the emotional, even the spiritual. When applied to theology, rationalism means the reduction of theology to mere propositions for debate. Theologians, according to rationalism, are scientists—no more and certainly no less.

As with any opposing views, pietism and rationalism spur each other on to more extreme positions. The pendulum swings further and further apart. When Dietrich Bonhoeffer began lecturing as a young professor of theology at the University of Berlin, he looked out on a room full of students bred in the ways of rationalism. When he looked out on the churches, especially the more conservative churches, he saw pews full of pietists. This was Bonhoeffer's context. As a theologian and a churchman, he had his work cut out for him.

Bonhoeffer sought to bring together what had been driven asunder. Into this division between spirituality and theology, the debates between the rationalists and pietists, Bonhoeffer forged a middle way, offering warnings to both extremes. He did this from two primary commitments. The first commitment is what has been said already, that *theology is in the service of the church*. The second commitment is that *theology must be lived out*. Theology always obligates us. Beliefs and confessions, the domain of theology, must be practiced, the domain of Christian living. To confess a belief is to live by, from, through, and for that belief. Theology and Christian living go together. The church as a whole and individual Christians suffer when we pit theology and spirituality or matters of Christian living against each other. We thrive when they work together.

Theology as Confession: Theology's Place in the Life of the Church

You might be thinking you've been tricked by the title of this chapter. The title "Confession" may have led you to think this chapter is about confessing our sins. That type of confession was crucial to Bonhoeffer. We can trace this back to Martin Luther, who traced it back to the Bible (James 5:16). Luther, even amid his break from the Roman Catholic Church, advocated confessing our sins to each other and to priests. In his Larger Catechism (1529) he offers instruction for such confession. Bonhoeffer follows suit.

During his days as director at the seminary at Finkenwalde, Bonhoeffer advocated confessing sins to God, obviously, but also regular times of private confession to each other. The students bucked this for a time, but despite their protests, Bonhoeffer kept up the practice. The confession of sin to each other was a significant part of Christian community for him. He was convinced that true fellowship cannot exist without it. After Finkenwalde, Bonhoeffer continued to advocate for confession in his writing of *Life Together*. While this type of confession plays a role in living the Christian life, it's not the subject of this chapter. Confession here means theology, *the confessing of belief in and about God*.

For Bonhoeffer this confessing of belief has a goal. Confession shapes our life. Theologians reflect, wrestle, argue, confess, pray, serve, and live—all in humble dependence upon the grace of God and in submission to the

Word of God. All of these are in a symbiotic relationship. This is what Bonhoeffer wanted for his seminarians, for his church, and for himself. You
can't have the Christian life or the church without confession.[1]

Confessions, or statements of faith, have a long history in the life of the
church. Some argue that confessions may even be found within the pages of
Scripture. Deuteronomy 6:4 smacks of a confession, albeit a brief one. Some
think 1 Timothy 3:16 is either a hymn or a confession that was circulating
in the early church and that Paul incorporated into his letter to his protégé.
Paul offers a rhythmic summary of Christ's earthly life in the passage, and
he introduces these lines with the words, "Great indeed, *we confess.*"

As we move out of the pages of the New Testament and on to the early
church, we see creeds and confessions of faith playing a crucial role. Even
before the end of the first century, bishops wrote up creeds for use in in-
structing new converts, reciting in public worship, and teaching the faithful. Over the centuries these early creeds of the bishops were synthesized
and developed, eventually leading to the Apostles' Creed, so named because it represents a summary of the apostolic teaching, which is to say,
the New Testament. In other words, it is a summary statement of Christian
doctrine.

In the early church, we also see the two great creeds stemming from
the ecumenical councils. Both the Nicene Creed (AD 325) and the Chalcedonian Creed (451) offer definitive statements on the biblical teaching of
the person and work of Christ, and the implications of this teaching for
church life. These creeds served as boundary markers, delineating the line
between heresy and orthodoxy. We learn from the early church how the
creeds grew out of the church's worship. Since believers gathered to worship Christ and celebrate his incarnation, crucifixion, and resurrection,
they needed to know exactly who Christ is. The urgency of that question,
the identity of Christ, drove the church to make creeds.

As we move into the time of Reformation, we see another cycle of creed
making, which also comes at a time of urgency in the church's life. The
leaders of the various branches of the Reformation set about writing down
their understanding of biblical teaching in light of questions such as the
nature of the gospel and the identity of the true church. The Reformers
sought to put down on paper their beliefs and then offer these statements

---

[1] For a compelling discussion of the need for confessions, see Carl R. Trueman, *The Creedal Imperative* (Wheaton, IL: Crossway, 2012).

to church members to keep them faithful to the Bible, to help them grow in their faith, and to assist them in the worship of God.

To this end, Luther both wrote catechisms, the Child's Catechism and the Larger Catechism (both in 1529), and, with help from others, wrote confessions, the Augsburg Confession (1530) and the Smalcald Articles (1537). After Luther's death came the Book of Concord (1577). These documents form the theological backbone of Lutheranism. The various Reformed and Presbyterian denominations, Anabaptist movements, and Baptist movements were all devoted to making creeds in the sixteenth and seventeenth centuries.[2]

In the twentieth century the various mainline denominations began drifting away from their moorings in these theological confessions from the Reformation era. For example, mainline and theologically liberal Presbyterians gave a diminished role to the Westminster Standards (comprising the Westminster Shorter and Larger Catechisms, the Westminster Confession of Faith, and the Directory for Public Worship), prompting criticisms from J. Gresham Machen and others in the 1920s and leading to the emergence of new denominations, including the eventual Presbyterian Church in America (PCA). Reformed churches in such denominations as the United Churches of Christ (UCC) turned away from their commitment to the Heidelberg Catechism (1563) and other confessions of the Reformation era, such as the Canons of the Synod of Dort (1618–1619). The ecumenical winds, accompanied by the ever-growing presence of modernist sensibilities, led these mainline denominations to reduce the role of their theological confessions in their church life.

The diminished role of confession in the mainline churches serves as a cautionary tale for more evangelical and theologically conservative constituencies. When theology is diminished—and sometimes theologians are the culprit in this—the church is living on borrowed capital. Once that is spent, the church faces a debt crisis. Drift comes in all shapes and sizes, sometimes subtle, sometimes overt, sometimes unintentional, sometimes intentional. But drift is always deadly.

This confessional drift was equaled by a scriptural drift, as the Bible also played a diminished role in church life in these mainline denominations in the twentieth century. As goes theology so goes the place of

---

[2] For a full discussion of the history of confessions, see Jaroslav Pelikan, *Credo: Historical and Theological Guide to Creeds and Confessions of Faith in the Christian Tradition* (New Haven, CT: Yale University Press, 2003).

the Bible, and, consequently, so goes the life and mission of the church. Such drifts may be seen throughout the battles within denominations in America and in Europe throughout the twentieth century.

And the Lutheran Church followed suit. When Bonhoeffer set up the seminary at Finkenwalde, he purposed to correct three deficiencies he saw plaguing the national church—deficiencies he was determined to avoid in the Confessing Church. The first deficiency was prayer, as in the lack of prayer and the lack of teaching on prayer. The second was the lack of reading, meditating upon, and interpreting the Bible. The third deficiency concerned lack of study of, teaching of, and commitment to the theological confessions of the Lutheran Church.

In previous chapters we explored what Bonhoeffer had to say about prayer and Scripture, and how he emphasized these in the curriculum of the seminary and in the personal and community life of the seminarians at Finkenwalde. Prayer and Bible reading are essential ingredients to the minister, his spiritual life, and the life of his church. In fact, there's no true church without them. Little wonder the national church had lost its way. Its ministers were deficient in the three essential ingredients for a healthy church—prayer, Scripture, and theology.

Bonhoeffer had an equal estimation of confession—of theological study and theological commitment. The German Lutheran Church, the Reich Church, in the early-to-mid-1930s was downplaying theology, not to mention Scripture. Bonhoeffer knew, though, that without rigorous theological reflection and commitment the church was selling its soul. Even though the national church had adopted a loose relationship with its creeds of the past, Bonhoeffer was determined that the ordinands at Finkenwalde would be thoroughly immersed in their confessional standards. For Bonhoeffer, theology, expressed in confession, mattered.

There Will Be Theology Here

Recalling life at Finkenwalde, Eberhard Bethge notes how "Bonhoeffer enjoyed spending time in the Smalcald Articles."[3] Bethge adds, "He loved the *Formula of Concord*."[4] And he based the curriculum around these documents. Bethge tells us:

---

[3] Eberhard Bethge, *Dietrich Bonhoeffer: A Biography*, enl. ed. (Minneapolis: Fortress, 2000), 447.
[4] Ibid., 449. *The Formula of Concord* (1557), Lutheranism's authoritative doctrinal confession, includes the Augsburg Confession. See www.bookofconcord.org.

Every page of the *Formula of Concord* in Bonhoeffer's copy of the confessional writings is covered with underlined passages, exclamation marks, and question marks. During the later courses at Finkenwalde these underlines, markings, and questions became the predominant theme in this series of lectures.[5]

We should appreciate the question marks. One of my church history professors and quite a churchman in his denomination, William S. Barker, used to relay his experiences in examining candidates for the ministry. In the Presbyterian Church in America, the doctrinal standards are the Westminster Confession, the Larger and Shorter Catechism, and the Directory for Public Worship. Candidates need to express their agreement with these standards in order to be ordained. Professor Barker expressed how he preferred candidates who had a list of scruples for discussion of the standards over candidates who simply signed off in full without any questions. He wondered whether this latter group had even read the doctrinal standards. Barker would enjoy Bonhoeffer's question marks. They show that Bonhoeffer was wrestling with the standards of the Lutheran Church, that he was taking seriously how these centuries-old standards lead and guide the church today. Someone who cares little for their denominational standards dismisses them or nods tacit approval to them. But someone who takes them seriously underlines them, marks them up, and asks questions.

Bonhoeffer grappled with his denomination's theological confession and he made sure his students would do the same. A few years earlier in a letter to Barth, Bonhoeffer expresses his frustration in the church struggles. "Our church regime," he writes, "totally lacks even the concept of heresy."[6] He would say the same things—though with a stronger tone—to his students in his lectures on christology from the same period: "For us the concept of heresy no longer exists . . . the word heresy has been struck from our vocabulary. And yet the concept of heresy is a necessary, nonnegotiable factor for the confessing church. Doctrine must always be set against false doctrine."[7] He quickly adds that this talk of heresy is out of love, not out of a lack of love. Not speaking the truth and not calling heresy *heresy* would be unloving, whereas, "if I do speak the truth to them, I'm doing it out of love."[8]

---

[5] Bethge, *Dietrich Bonhoeffer*, 449.
[6] Bonhoeffer to Karl Barth, September 9, 1933, *DBWE* 12:165.
[7] Bonhoeffer, "Lectures on Christology," *DBWE* 12:332.
[8] Ibid.

In 1933 Bonhoeffer recognized significant theological problems in his church, and yet he found himself unable to engage in theological debate. This inability had nothing to do with him. It stemmed from his church's dismissal of theology, as its leaders had not even the concept of heresy. At Finkenwalde, Bonhoeffer made sure both concepts—theology and heresy—would be rightly understood and eminently conspicuous.

Actually, Bonhoeffer had insisted on such while he was teaching at Berlin. Prior to taking up his post there, he spent a year at Union Theological Seminary. The academic year of 1929–1930 was a crucial time in American Christianity. In 1929 Machen resigned from Princeton Theological Seminary and founded Westminster Theological Seminary, which opened its doors on September 25 of that year. These were the tumultuous days of the clash between fundamentalists and liberals. Union Seminary was a flagship in the liberal fleet, with no less than Harry Emerson Fosdick on board for homiletics. And Bonhoeffer was there at Union to see and hear it all.

Bonhoeffer prepared a written report of his year at Union for the Church Federation Office in Germany. He pulls no punches when he writes, "The theological spirit at Union Theological Seminary is accelerating the process of secularization of Christianity in America."[9] He continues,

> A seminary in which numerous students openly laugh during a public lecture because they find it amusing when a passage on sin and forgiveness from Luther's *On the Bondage of the Will* is cited has obviously, despite its many advantages, forgotten what Christian theology in its very essence stands for.[10]

He later adds, "In a discussion before numerous students, one of the leading professors at Union Theological Seminary confessed to me amid the applause of the students that justification by faith was not only unimportant but also a matter of indifference to him."[11]

During Bonhoeffer's year in New York City, he managed to travel by car to Mexico, all around the East Coast, and down even to the Florida Keys. He also made it to Cuba, where he spent the Christmas holiday. While there, he wrote to his superintendent, Max Diestel, about "the sad part of the whole thing" at Union Theological Seminary. Bonhoeffer says plainly, "There is no

[9] Bonhoeffer, "Report on His Year of Study Prepared for the Church Federation Office," 1931, *DBWE* 10:309.
[10] Ibid., 309–10.
[11] Ibid., 311.

theology here."[12] If Bonhoeffer learned anything from his time at Union, it was this: wherever he would go on to teach, he would make sure that there would be theology there.

Theology in the Service of the Church

He was interested in theology of a particular kind, however. The theology Bonhoeffer had in mind was a theology for the church—not merely a theology that speaks *to* the church, but a theology that *serves* the church. It's no coincidence that Bonhoeffer discovered both an absence of theology at Union and an absence of preaching in the churches whose pulpits would be filled with Union or like-minded seminary graduates. If he could say of Union, "There's no theology here," he could say and did say, "There's no sermon here" as he visited church after church. Of Riverside Cathedral, Fosdick's church, Bonhoeffer could only write in his diary on June 18, 1939, "Simply unbearable."[13]

The very next Sunday he visited a church of his own denomination, a Lutheran church along Central Park. Of the sermon that day he notes how little gospel there was, how little exegesis of the text, and how flat the whole thing was. "It is very pathetic," he concludes.[14] And a Sunday later he visited a Methodist church. This sermon was "without a text" and had "not the faintest echo of Christian proclamation."[15] Then he boarded a ship and headed home. On board he attended a church service, held by an American pastor, of which Bonhoeffer records, "the sermon sentimental and full of hollow phrases."[16] These were sermons, four in a row, quite literally not worth writing home about.

During a short visit to Lakeville, Connecticut, in 1939 he commented that he got more out of watching "thousands of fireflies" (lightning bugs) than he did in those sermons. Without good theology it only follows there would not be a true sermon. Bonhoeffer was experiencing the best American liberalism had to offer.

A theology that best serves the church has two essential and defining characteristics: it faithfully expresses God's revelation, and it serves the

---

[12] Bonhoeffer to Max Diestel, December 19, 1930, *DBWE* 10: 265. He will later say in a letter to Diestel, once his courses have ended, "My course of study here at the seminary . . . did not yield very much," April 25, 1931, *DBWE* 10:296.
[13] Bonhoeffer, "American Diary," June 18, 1939, *DBWE* 15:224.
[14] Bonhoeffer, "American Diary," June 25, 1939, *DBWE* 15:231.
[15] Bonhoeffer, "American Diary," July 2, 1939, *DBWE* 15:236.
[16] Bonhoeffer, "American Diary," July 9, 1939, *DBWE* 15:238.

church. To put this second characteristic another way, a theology that best serves the church is a theology that preaches. In earlier chapters we looked at a piece Bonhoeffer wrote in 1940, his lecture outline "Theology and the Congregation." There he reminds us that the church "is built solely on the word of God."[17] He adds:

> Theology is submission to the coherent and well-ordered knowledge of the word of God in its context and in its particular form as guided by the confessions of the church. It serves the pure proclamation of the word in the congregation and the building up of the congregation in accord with the word of God.[18]

Bonhoeffer goes on to note how the congregation needs clarity. It needs clarity regarding the Word of God and clarity regarding what is true and what is false. That's where confession and the work of the theologian-pastor makes the entrance.[19] From such preaching of the Word comes faith, and from such faith comes life.

Just before he wrote this piece in 1940, he sent a Christmas meditation to his scattered former students and the young pastors in the Confessing Church. He was struck by the mystery of the incarnation and used that event and the occasion of Christmas to remind his students of the role of mystery in faith. He says what foolishness it is "to decode God's mystery, pulling it down to the commonplace, miracle-less words of wisdom based on human experience and reason!"[20] Here he defines the theologian's task as "to comprehend, defend, and exalt the mystery of God, precisely as mystery."[21] The task of clarity is never at the expense of mystery. But it's not enough to simply "fall back" on mystery at every turn, either. We put both of these pieces together to see the balance in the theologian's task of both clarity and mystery in the preaching of God's Word. The incarnation, the subject of Bonhoeffer's Christmas letter, stands as a salient example of this combination of clarity and mystery.

The incarnation, what Bonhoeffer speaks of as being a crucial piece to the "edifice of Christology," has long been the focus of the work of theo-

---

[17] Bonhoeffer, "Theology and the Congregation," 1940, *DBWE* 16:494.
[18] Ibid.
[19] For more on this particular point, see John Piper and D. A. Carson, *The Pastor as Scholar and the Scholar as Pastor: Reflections on Life and Ministry*, ed. David Mathis and Owen Strachan (Wheaton, IL: Crossway, 2011).
[20] Bonhoeffer, "Meditation on Christmas," December 1939, *DBWE* 15:529.
[21] Ibid.

logians. Bonhoeffer commends such work and its carefully constructed framework. But he concludes his letter with this observation:

> But the point, of course, is not that we admire this edifice, but that through one or another of these thoughts we will be led to read and contemplate the biblical testimony to the mystery of God's becoming human with more reverence and adoration, and perhaps even to sing Luther's Christmas hymns more thoughtfully and joyously.[22]

So there we have, according to Bonhoeffer, the theologian's complex task in constructing a theology that preaches, a theology in service of the church. The theologian offers the church both clarity and mystery that leads to reverence and adoration of God. It also leads to joy, a joy that would not otherwise come so readily to underground pastors and seminarians on the brink of the unleashing of the Nazi war machine. That is a theology that preaches.

Conclusion: Theology in Life

A theology that preaches is ultimately a theology for life. Thoughtful reflection, reverence, adoration, and joy all lead to life—a certain kind of life, the life of discipleship. Perhaps nowhere in Bonhoeffer's writings is this seen more acutely than in his closing chapter of *The Cost of Discipleship*. The whole book actually represents this rich blend of deep theological reflection with earthy, real-life application; but here in the last chapter, entitled "The Image of Christ," Bonhoeffer brings the two parts into perfect harmony.

As he concludes the chapter and the classic book on the Christian life, he observes, "The follower [*Nachfolger*] of Jesus is the imitator [*Nachahmer*] of God."[23] In the chapter, Bonhoeffer offers pastoral clarity in reflecting on how Christ bore the image of God perfectly, how Christ *is* the image of God perfectly (2 Cor. 4:4). Bonhoeffer takes us back to Adam, created in God's image. But then Adam fell. So Bonhoeffer laments that human beings "live now without their essential purpose, that of being the image of God. Human beings live without being truly human. They must live without being able to live. That is the paradox of our existence and the source of all our woes."[24] But then he sounds a joyful note: "God sends God's son—that

---

[22] *DBWE* 15:533.
[23] *DBWE* 4:288.
[24] *DBWE* 4:282.

is the only way to find help."[25] Christ comes. But he comes in an image
that, Bonhoeffer observes, is quite different from the image in Adam in the
glories of Paradise:

> It is the image of one who places himself in the very midst of the world of
> sin and death, who takes on the needs of human flesh, who humbly sub-
> mits to God's wrath and judgment over sinners, who remains obedient to
> God's will in suffering and death; the one born in poverty, who befriended
> and sat at table to eat with tax collectors and sinners, and who, on the
> cross, was rejected by God and human beings—this is God in human
> form, this is the human being who is the new image of God.[26]

In short, Christ is the image of the crucified life, and that is the life we
are called to live. Bonhoeffer cites Galatians 2:20, "It is no longer I who live,
but it is Christ who lives in me," then adds, "The incarnate, crucified, and
transfigured one has entered into me and lives my life."[27] So discipleship is
bearing his image, walking as he walked, serving as he served, loving as he
loved, forgiving as he forgave.[28] We lose our lives in Christ, and in following
him and imitating him we find our lives.[29] We, because of sin, did not live;
now we, because of Christ, live.

This approach to discipleship, to living the Christian life, flows from
theology and the theological contemplation of both the first image bearer,
Adam, and the last and ultimate image bearer, Christ. By framing theology
around image bearing, Bonhoeffer directly and unmistakenly connects
theology to life, theology to discipleship, theology to Christian living.
There is no pitting of theology against Christian living. Rather, Bonhoeffer teaches, and his life demonstrates, that theology and Christian living
must go together.

---

[25] *DBWE* 4:283.
[26] *DBWE* 4:284.
[27] *DBWE* 4:287.
[28] *DBWE* 4:287.
[29] *DBWE* 4:287–88.

PART 4

LIFE

If we want to have Christ, we must recognize that he makes crucial claims on our entire lives. We understand him not if we make room for him in merely one province of our spiritual life, but only if our life takes its orientation from him alone. . . . The religion of Christ is not the tidbit after the bread; it is the bread itself, or it is nothing.

DIETRICH BONHOEFFER,
LECTURE, "JESUS CHRIST AND
THE ESSENCE OF CHRISTIANITY,"
BARCELONA, 1928

CHAPTER 7

WORLDLINESS

The difference between the Christian hope of resurrection and the mythological hope is that the former sends a man back to his life on earth in a wholly new way. . . . The Christian, unlike the devotees of the redemption myths, has no line of escape available from earthly tasks and difficulties. . . . But, like Christ himself—"My God, why hast thou forsaken me?"—he must drink the earthly cup to the dregs, and only in his doing so is the crucified and risen Lord with him, and he crucified and risen with Christ. This world must not be prematurely written off.

DIETRICH BONHOEFFER,
FROM TEGEL PRISON, 1944

Thinking back to the teaching I received on living the Christian life, I never once remember hearing "worldliness" put in a positive light. Instead, worldliness ranked with the deadliest of poisons. A giant "Mr. Yuk" sticker, that's the image I associate with worldliness.

Along comes Dietrich Bonhoeffer advocating a worldly discipleship. Shocking! Perhaps in Bonhoeffer no two phrases sound more foreign or laced with more problems than his "religionless Christianity" and "worldly discipleship." The second one concerns us here. According to John's first epistle, among other places in Scripture, worldliness stands as one of three enemies of the Christian, teamed up with the flesh and Satan. Paul says flatly, "Do not be conformed to this world" (Rom. 12:2). Avoid worldliness at all costs. So what are we to make of Bonhoeffer's call to a life of worldliness? We start with what he means by it.

Of Monks and Cultural Protestants

In Christ's final moments with the disciples before the cross, recorded in John 17, he asks the Father not to take the disciples out of the world (17:15). He prays straightforwardly that his followers will be in the world. In fact, Christ has "sent them into the world" (17:18). He also notes, however, that his disciples are "not of the world" (17:16). And so we have the succinct statement of our relationship to the world as Christ's disciples: *in the world, but not of the world.* Though it's a succinct phrase and clear enough on the surface, living it out and understanding how it is lived out in particular situations and contexts is another matter altogether.

In the previous century, H. Richard Niebuhr referred to this challenge of being in the world but not of it as "the enduring problem," and he wrote his classic text *Christ and Culture* to address the question.[1] Niebuhr partly answered the problem by exploring the various approaches throughout Christian history. Over the centuries, Christians have been all over the continuum of being in the world and not of it. And, not surprisingly, various movements and individuals tend to be better at one or the other. That is to say, we rarely get the balance right between being in the world but not of it. We're much better at the extremes of one or the other.

Bonhoeffer reduced the positions along the continuum to two groups: monks (the "not of the world" emphasis) and cultural Protestants (the "in the world" emphasis).[2] His own Germany has a rich tradition of both. Luther once quipped, "God placed his church in the midst of the world, among countless external activities and callings, not in order that Christians should become monks but so that they may live in fellowship and that our works and the exercises of our faith may become known among them."[3] A former monk himself, Luther was rather fond of criticizing the monastery. In his view, the monastery drew Christians away from their calling to be salt and light in the world, not to mention Luther's observation of the lack of biblical warrant for celibacy.

By Bonhoeffer's day, the pendulum had swung over to the other ex-

---

[1] H. Richard Niebuhr, *Christ and Culture* (New York: Harper & Row, 1956).
[2] *DBWE* 6:57.
[3] Martin Luther, "Table Talk, No. 3993," August 31, 1538, in *Luther's Works*, vol. 54, *Table Talk*, ed. and trans. Theodore G. Tappert (Philadelphia: Fortress, 1967), 307.

treme. His was a day and a church rife with cultural Protestants, who had lost the distinction of being salt and were not all that bright as lights. Against these two swings of the pendulum from the monastic form of Christianity to that of the cultural Protestant variety, Bonhoeffer called the church to a genuine worldly discipleship and a costly discipleship. I would venture that we understand Bonhoeffer's view of discipleship best by seeing it as "christotelic discipleship." This expression is not intended to be theological jargon. *Christotelic* comes from two words, *Christ* and the Greek word *telos*, which means end or purpose or design. The word helps us grasp what Bonheoffer sees as the true nature of discipleship. It basically means that we live *toward Christ*. This is the Christ-centered life, the life aimed at Christ like an arrow from an expert archer. This and the next two chapters intend to shed light on this expression, "christotelic discipleship."

Bonhoeffer will come to address this alternative to monasticism and to cultural Protestantism in *The Cost of Discipleship* and *Ethics*, and in numerous letters and shorter writings during his imprisonment. Perhaps he addresses this issue most directly in *Ethics*.

Ethics is an incomplete book published posthumously in 1949 in German, with a first English translation appearing in 1955. Bonhoeffer worked on it intermittently from 1941 through 1943. Despite his imprisonment, he managed to complete a large part of it. A sad line from one of the prison letters to Bethge finds Bonhoeffer lamenting, "I sometimes feel as if my life were more or less over, and as if all I had to do now were to finish my *Ethics*."[4] He did not, however, get to finish it. That imprisonment and the events of the 1940s conspired against the book's completion. Despite its unfinished nature, Bonhoeffer scholars declare *Ethics* Bonhoeffer's magnum opus, his great work. Bonhoeffer himself thought it to be his most important book.[5]

It builds on his previous work, especially *The Cost of Discipleship* (published in 1937) and his two books on the Christian community, *Sanctorum Communio* (written in 1927, published in 1930) and *Life Together* (published in 1939). Bonhoeffer must have been an interesting prisoner. In a letter to his prison interrogator, Dr. Roeder, Bonhoeffer offers an explanation of his travels and activities during the time of the "alleged" conspiratorial efforts. He brings up his *Ethics*, explaining that while his previous work

---

[4] Bonhoeffer to Eberhard Bethge, December 15, 1943, *LPP*, 163.
[5] Bonhoeffer to the judge advocate, Dr. Roeder, June 1941, *LPP*, 57.

for the church consisted mainly of being an academic theologian, in this
current project his focus concerns "a concrete evangelical ethics." That is
Bonhoeffer's defense, that he was too occupied with writing *Ethics* to be
involved in conspiracies.

When Bonhoeffer speaks of an *"evangelical* ethics," he's referring to the
Lutheran Church (the *Evangelische Kirche* in German). The question of how
we live in the world as Christians and as the church takes center stage in
the book. Bonhoeffer will come to call this living "responsible lives."[6]

Before we explore the contours of Bonhoeffer's responsible living and
christotelic discipleship, we need to look at the context of his work on this
topic from 1932 until the expression of his final thoughts in late 1944. As
we do, we come to see the role that context (or culture) plays in our thinking
about and living out theology and the Christian life.

Villains and Saints—in Plain Sight

We live the Christian life in context—not in the abstract and not in a vacuum. This is a truism Dietrich Bonhoeffer knew all too well. In the beginning of his *Ethics* he mentions that we simply cannot afford the luxury of
speaking of ethics in the abstract and the theoretical. There was an urgency
that left no room for mere theory. Bonhoeffer puts it this way: "Today we
have villains and saints again, in full public view. The gray on gray of a
sultry, rainy day has turned into the black cloud and bright lightning flash
of a thunderstorm. The contours are sharply drawn. Reality is laid bare.
Shakespeare's characters are among us."[7]

Bonhoeffer wrote and lived in his Shakespearean world, the only difference being that Bonhoeffer's world included air raids. It was Bonhoeffer's context. And you feel the sharp pinch of that context as you read his
book and as you watch the final decade or so of his life.

We also live in a culture, albeit a different context from that of Bonhoeffer. Too often we approach the Christian life as if it were isolated from
the ebb and flow of culture and of contexts. Bonhoeffer was concerned that
too many churchmen and philosophers approached ethics as mere theory.
He could not see tackling the subject apart from practice. So it is with the
way we sometimes engage discipleship. We like to talk in the abstract,

---

[6] See Clifford J. Green, "Editor's Introduction," *DBWE* 6:1–44, for a full discussion of the writing of *Ethics*
and its role in Bonhoeffer's thought. See also Robin W. Lovin's review of this volume, "Ethics for This
World," *The Christian Century* (April 19, 2005): 26–31.
[7] *DBWE* 6:76.

when in fact we live—whether we acknowledge it or not—in the concrete. What we need, as a consequence, is an approach to the Christian life that is fully aware of and fully engaged with our contexts. Bonhoeffer's single word to express this type of engagement was *worldliness*. He called for a genuine worldly discipleship, even speaking of a genuine Christianity as one that is nothing less than a "full-blown worldliness."[8]

An unbridled and unfettered "worldliness," for Bonhoeffer, is the only way to live the Christian life. What exactly does he mean? How can this approach to the Christian life help us?

In earlier chapters we learned how we live the Christian life *in Christ* and *in community*. Here we learn that we live the Christian life *in culture*. We live in rough and ready contexts, not in cool closets of abstractions and theories. We live, even as Christ told us in John 17, in the world. First, we need to come to grips with where we are.

Discipleship, or living the Christian life, is largely a matter of understanding what it means to be in the world but not of it, as we have already mentioned. I would also add that when it comes to living in the world, we need to remember the particular space and time *in which we live*. We live in our particular context. Sometimes we pine away in nostalgic rapture for some bygone time in some distant place.

I came of age during the standoff between the United States and the Soviet Union, the infamous era of the Cold War. In the late 1970s and early 1980s, prior to Glasnost and the end of the Cold War, I heard many stirring stories of the persecution and arrest of Christians behind the Iron Curtain. As a young Christian I distinctly remember how inferior I felt compared to the testimonies of these brothers and sisters in Christ, thinking I was a far lesser Christian than they. I could not see then that I was called to be a disciple in my own context, not theirs, that my own context provided challenges and opportunities, and that my call was to be faithful in light of those.

Wishing I was somewhere else did not accomplish much at all. For that matter, we would not accomplish much by comparing our lives to that of Bonhoeffer. But we could accomplish much by learning from him *the importance of living out our Christian calling in the place in which God has called us to live and to work and to serve.* We need to be disciples not only in the world, but in that particular slice of the world in which God has placed us.

This is a key part of living the Christian life as it bumps into the notion

---

[8] *DBWE* 6:401.

of contentment. We think others have it so much easier. Or we think if only our circumstances were changed to this or that, *then* we could really start to live the Christian life. While it's true that we sometimes need to challenge the status quo and not merely accept things because "that's the way they are," it's also true that we need to be faithful where God has placed us. If anyone could make excuses, Bonhoeffer could. He was in prison, separated from his fiancée, cut off from his family and friends, and his career stopped short just when, at the age of thirty-seven, academics tend only to start revving up for their careers and contributions. Bonhoeffer certainly could have made excuses, but he didn't.

As we see in his prison writings, however, he had learned to be content and faithful in that very context. "You must never doubt that I'm traveling with gratitude and cheerfulness along the road where I'm being led," he writes to his dear friend, Eberhard. "My life is brim-full of God's goodness, and my sins are covered by the forgiving love of Christ crucified."[9] So how can we have such contentment in the place in which God has called us to be his disciple?

Two Worlds Collide

The answer starts with taking us back to the continuum of models that target either being "in the world" or being "not of the world." We can't have an either–or here and still be faithful to Christ's calling on our lives. We must have a both–and. Let's first explore the strong pull of going in the either–or direction. It's helpful to see where we can go wrong in order to see where we can go right.

There is much confusion over how to live in the world. It wasn't just during the Middle Ages, with Bonhoeffer's "monks," or the beginnings of modernity, with Bonhoeffer's "cultural Protestants," that missteps were taken regarding Christ's call to be in the world but not of it. We too make many missteps in our attempts to be faithful to this foundational call as disciples of Christ. We stumble along in our discipleship. We stumble in our own Christian life, in our relationships, in our marriages and our parenting, and in our life in our Christian communities. Many times our stumbling is due to a faulty view of the world, like walking a dangerous trail while wearing the wrong glasses.

---

[9] Bonhoeffer to Eberhard Bethge, August 23, 1944, *LPP*, 393.

The monk sees only danger in the world, where temptations abound. Like John Bunyan's "Christian" being plopped down in Vanity Fair, we must stick our fingers in our ears, says the monk, close our eyes, and run away with abandon. Better to live in a monastery than to be swept away by temptation. Better to isolate yourself than risk falling into sin. This view suffers from, among other things, a negative view of culture. To put the matter another way, an approach to the Christian life obsessed with avoiding worldliness sits at odds with not only the negative elements of the world, but also the world itself. It affirms a position of withdrawing from culture, standing back from it, and abstaining from participating in it. It enters the monastery.

Scripture itself offers a more complex view of the world. It speaks of the world in positive ways—as in various psalms—not just negative tones. As the hymn writer Maltbie Babcock put it, "This Is My Father's World." James, after his stern warnings of temptation, speaks of good gifts coming down from heaven (James 1:17). Paul celebrates the good things that were created by God and actually rebukes those who promote a monasticism of abstaining from marriage and forbidding certain foods (1 Tim. 4:1–3). Instead, he commends, "Everything created by God is good, and nothing is to be rejected if it is received with thanksgiving, for it is made holy by the word of God and prayer" (1 Tim. 4:4–5).[10] This perspective on the world and culture needs to be seen as a corrective to a negative view and a concomitant unhealthy withdrawal from the world.

But what about the pull in the other direction, the pull to be "of the world"? This is what Bonhoeffer called "cultural Protestant," going in the exact opposite direction of the monk. This view doesn't spend much time with 1 John's warnings to avoid worldliness. In short, this view downplays the fall and gives short shrift to sin, missing Christ's admonition to be not of the world. Bonhoeffer will come to call this cheap grace. Among the opening pages of *The Cost of Discipleship*, he says, "The expression of Christianity and the increasing secularization of the church caused the awareness of costly grace to be gradually lost."[11] Almost a decade later he writes to Bethge of "the banal this-worldliness of the enlightened, the busy, the comfortable, or the lascivious."[12] Bonhoeffer aims this laundry list at the church, at pastors and at theologians, not at people generally or those outside of the church. The

---

[10] Some commentators think the phrase "made holy by the word of God" refers back to the creation, specifically to the creation of all things by divine fiat, by divine speech. This would mean there is goodness in God's creation inherently, sourced in God and his creative act.

[11] *DBWE* 4:46.

[12] Bonhoeffer to Eberhard Bethge, July 21, 1944, *LPP*, 369.

enlightened, busy, comfortable, or lascivious have all made themselves too at home in the world. They take God's Word too lightly.

Bonhoeffer has in mind here a culturally accommodated Christianity, one that asks little of its adherents. Like the rich young ruler, they think a formal encounter with Jesus is enough as they go on their way and live as they please (Matt. 19:16–30). Bonhoeffer says of the rich young ruler that he well represents those who look for consolation, but "sought to console themselves with a forgiveness that they grant themselves"; they are caught up in an "entanglement with themselves."[13] Consequently they look, as the rich young ruler did, to a good teacher for advice, for suggestions. They do not seek, as Christ gives this representative person, "a divine order with unconditional authority."[14] They seek a guru to give them "peace of mind."

Bonhoeffer's novel *Sunday*, discussed back in chapter 3, was chock-full of such characters, and all to the perturbance of Frau Brake. Bonhoeffer has little time for these culturally accommodated churchgoers as well. He tends to simply call them the "religious," who follow a safe God who demands little. In our day, Christian Smith has termed this Moralistic Therapeutic Deism.[15]

The pull of being a cultural Protestant is comfort, but in the end it is a false comfort. Luther, borrowing a line from the prophet, declares in thesis 92 of his Ninety-Five Theses, "Away then with all those prophets who say to the people of Christ, 'Peace, peace,' and there is no peace!"[16] To respond to these two temptations—monkish withdrawal or an accommodating Protestantism—we need to step back and look at the world altogether differently. Bonhoeffer first brings clarity, then offers us some chastening remarks about the world and our living in it. Before we do step back for a better view, however, we need to look a bit more closely at Bonhoeffer's criticism of German Protestantism. This criticism would eventually lead him to call for a "religionless Christianity."

"Religionless Christianity"

We have seen that probably no phrase of Bonhoeffer's has caused more consternation than his "religionless Christianity." All sides of the theologi-

---

[13] *DBWE* 4:69.
[14] *DBWE* 4:70.
[15] See Christian Smith and Melinda Lundquist Denton, *Soul Searching: The Religious and Spiritual Lives of American Teenagers* (New York: Oxford University Press, 2005).
[16] Martin Luther, *Martin Luther's Ninety-Five Theses*, ed. Stephen J. Nichols (Philipsburg, NJ: P&R, 2002), 47. The citation is rooted in Jer. 6:14 and 8:11, as well as in Ezek. 13:10 and 13:16.

cal spectrum, from Karl Barth to conservative American theologians, have taken issue with the phrase. So it demands our attention.

Bethge begins his lengthy discussion of the phrase by noting that this was not something that came to Bonhoeffer at Tegel, but may be traced back to his earlier writings. From the time of his early lectures at Berlin, Bonhoeffer used the word *religion* to refer to the Enlightenment's effort to replace faith. He puts the blame squarely at the feet of the English deists (including John Locke, though he's not mentioned by name): "In the world after Copernicus, under the influence of the English deists the word *religio* takes the place of 'faith.'"[17] Bonhoeffer proceeds to show how this marked a move away from the Reformation, which stressed faith. This is the first point in understanding what Bonhoeffer meant by "religionless Christianity." As Bethge summarizes it, "The diametrically opposite distinction between faith and religion was among his fundamental experiences."[18]

This move away from the Reformation, which stressed God's reaching down to us, led to a "Copernican revolution" of itself in which human beings now reached up to God. This would eventuate in the history of religions school (*Religionsgeschichtliche Schule*) in nineteenth-century Germany. To condense a long story, a few generations later the German Lutheran Church had lost its way. Bonhoeffer saw no hope in the formal, national church. He saw no hope in *religion*. And, while at Tegel, he proposed to abandon the church, which he saw as *religion*, in order to obtain a church that was faithful to God's Word and to Christ. Faith means God reaching down to us. Religion means humanity reaching up to God. Bonhoeffer cared only for the former and had no interest in the latter.

Bethge expands this thought of Bonhoeffer's when he writes, "What was meant here by 'religion' was that human activity which seeks to reach the beyond, to postulate a divinity, to invoke help and protection, in short: religion as self-justification."[19] Nothing appealed less to Bonhoeffer.

If we look back at Bonhoeffer's Berlin lectures, we see the implications of this move from faith to religion. Think of them as two chains of dominoes. After the initial domino of either faith or religion comes how one views the Bible, then how one views Christ, then the gospel, then the kingdom, and then ethics and discipleship. The chain having religion as the first domino forces you to see the Bible as a human book, Christ as only human and only

---

[17] Bonhoeffer, "The History of Twentieth-Century Systematic Theology," *DBWE* 11:209.
[18] Eberhard Bethge, *Dietrich Bonhoeffer: A Biography*, enl. ed. (Minneapolis: Fortress, 2000), 872.
[19] Ibid.

a good example, the gospel as devoid of justification, the kingdom as solely social betterment, and discipleship as nothing but self-fulfillment and self-actualization. Now we see why no such church or imitation of Christianity appealed to Bonhoeffer. This significant and tragic theological deficit also reveals how the German Lutheran Church (the *Reichskirche*) was powerless to speak against Hitler and impotent before him.

But if we look at the other domino train, which starts with faith, we get an entirely different outcome. When we start with faith, we see the Bible as God's word revealed to us. Next, we see Christ as the God-man, who died for us and in our place. Next, we see the gospel as necessarily meaning justification, stressing how passive we are in salvation. Then we see the kingdom as the reversal of the curse and the reestablishment of *shalom*. Finally, we see discipleship as following Jesus, the life of learning of the fellowship of his sufferings and the power of his resurrection. Bonhoeffer would take faith over religion any day.

Bethge offers an understatement: "At the end Bonhoeffer arrived at a stage that was highly critical of the church."[20] Eric Metaxas chimes in, "This 'religious' Christianity had failed Germany and the West during this great time of crisis, for one thing, and [Bonhoeffer] wondered whether it wasn't finally time for the lordship of Jesus Christ to move past Sunday mornings and churches and into the whole world."[21] Religion was too small, too confining, and, consequently, far too unhelpful. Bonhoeffer decided to look elsewhere. He looked back to faith, which led him back to a Christ-centered or, as we have been saying, a christotelic Christianity.[22]

In the Berlin lectures, after Bonhoeffer's observation of the move from faith to religion, he proceeds to focus on Christ and his work, stressing justification and the alien righteousness that, flowing from the cross, reaches down to us.[23] Much of Western Protestantism did not have room for this teaching as it was consumed with self-justification. Hence, we have Bonhoeffer's criticism and his proposal to move in an entirely different direction.

At Tegel, Bonhoeffer continued to develop his idea of religionless Christianity, though he never got the opportunity to develop it fully. In a letter to Bethge, Bonhoeffer explains, "What keeps gnawing at me is the

[20] Ibid., 887.
[21] Eric Metaxas, *Bonhoeffer: Pastor, Martyr, Prophet, Spy* (Nashville: Thomas Nelson, 2010), 467.
[22] Bethge, curiously, lets on that Bonhoeffer's christology was far too much for Barth to handle, which is why Barth did not see anything helpful in pursuing Bonhoeffer's "religionless Christianity" proposal. See Bethge, *Dietrich Bonhoeffer*, 888–90.
[23] Ibid., 236–39.

question, 'What is Christianity, or who is Christ actually for us today?'"[24] Religious language won't answer that question, or it won't answer the question well enough. To answer it, Bonhoeffer looks to Christ and sees the God who suffers, the God of weakness, the themes we bumped into back in chapter 2. Bonhoeffer had seen the world, at least the Western world, come of age and jettison God. Then he saw the world plunge into World War II. From his prison cell, he was thinking of how he, and how the church, could again speak to the world. Pious answers and religious formality wouldn't do. That much Bonhoeffer knew for certain. In another letter to Bethge he mentions how he is thinking about the concepts of repentance, faith, justification, rebirth, and sanctification "in the sense of John 1:14."[25] He's thinking of how the church lost its way by losing sight of Christ, and he's thinking about how to help the church find its way back. Bonhoeffer might have caused less of a stir had he spoken of a "Christ-full Christianity" instead of a "religionless Christianity." But when you understand what he meant by it, you begin to see how right he was.[26]

The One Reality

Bonhoeffer's Christ-full vision not only helps us understand the role of the church, but also helps us understand how we live in the world. Bonhoeffer looks beneath the surface of these labels and even beneath the surface of the actions of either the monk or the cultural Protestant to see faulty worldviews at the source and root of the problem. In an early chapter in *Ethics* labeled "Christ, Reality, and Good," Bonhoeffer speaks of faulty concepts of reality that drive a sharp wedge between the "real world," the physical or natural realm, and the spiritual or heavenly realm. He lays the blame at the feet of thinkers from the Middle Ages, arguing, "The whole of medieval history turned around the theme of the spiritual realm over the worldly, the *regnum gratiae* over the *regnum naturae*."[27] Of course, the advent of modernity triggered the reversal of fortunes. The realm of nature increasingly

---

[24] Bonhoeffer to Eberhard Bethge, April 30, 1944, *DBWE* 8:362.

[25] Bonhoeffer to Eberhard Bethge, May 5, 1944, *DBWE* 8:373.

[26] Bonhoeffer scholar Christian Gremmels concludes his discussion of Bonhoeffer's "religionless Christianity" by noting, "In summary, Bonhoeffer's theme is *not* the 'coming of age,' 'this-worldliness,' and 'religionlessness' of the modern world. As plausible and impressive as these expressions are, theologically they function only as auxiliary concepts. They serve the task of witnessing to Jesus Christ in the present," "Editor's Afterword to the German Edition," *DBWE* 8:588.

[27] *DBWE* 6:57. *Regnum gratiae* means the reign or realm of grace, the spiritual realm, while *regnum naturae* means the reign or realm of nature. The editors of *Ethics* explain that Bonhoeffer means to include by these expressions "a spatial component," as in a place. We could say these represent both two different places and two different worldviews.

pushed the spiritual realm to the margins. The real world, as it were, took up more and more space, leaving a smaller and smaller place for the spiritual. Bonhoeffer puts it this way: "The modern age is characterized by an ever-progressing independence of the worldly over against the spiritual."[28] Theism gave way to deism as it gave way to naturalism.

Bonhoeffer does not advocate a return to the medieval way. In fact, he sees the tug-of-war between the spiritual and the natural as the precise point of the problem. Either we become the monk, totally engrossed in the spiritual *at the expense of* engaging the world, or we become the cultural Protestant, totally engrossed in the natural *at the expense of* taking Christ seriously. Or we have a third option: "try to stand in the two realms at the same time" and in the process become a "people in eternal conflict."[29]

Living in the Real World

None of these three options appeals to Bonhoeffer. So he goes back to the root of the problem, which he sees as the distinction between the two realms, the two realities of the spiritual and the natural. He argues, "There are not two realities, but *only one reality*, and that is God's reality revealed in Christ in the reality of the world."[30] Typical of German thinkers, Bonhoeffer runs a few separate words together to create a single German word to express his view: *Christuswirklichkeit*, a compound that means the one realm of *the Christ-reality*.[31] This requires us to have a fundamentally different perspective on the world than we tend to take. It does not solve all the problems of living "in the world but not of it," to be sure, but it is a good place to start thinking about how to pull it off.

The answer that we should give to the modern world, to Bonhoeffer's "cultural Protestant," is not "Make room for Christ." Nor should we say to Bonhoeffer's monk, "Make room for the world." Instead both need a radically different perspective, a unified perspective of the singular Christ-reality. We need that same perspective to see both the claims Christ makes on our lives as his disciples and how every aspect of our lives comes to be conscripted in our discipleship.

A twenty-two-year-old Bonhoeffer expressed this line of thinking in a lecture he gave while in Barcelona, entitled "Jesus Christ and the Essence

[28] *DBWE* 6:57.
[29] *DBWE* 6:58.
[30] *DBWE* 6:58, emphasis his.
[31] *DBWE* 6:58.

of Christianity." Bonhoeffer addresses the tradition of critical scholarship that differentiated between the historical Jesus and the Jesus of faith, the so-called "Quest for the Historical Jesus." To distance himself from this approach altogether, Bonhoeffer states, "We allow the New Testament truly to speak, and for once we are listeners, hearing the claim this book presents in its entire power."[32] This involves our submitting to God's Word and not, as the "Quest" has it, submitting God's Word to us. We must listen to God's Word in this way. As Bonhoeffer observes, "If we want to have [Christ], we must recognize that he makes crucial claims on our entire lives. We understand him not if we make room for him in merely one province of our spiritual life, but only if our life takes its orientation from him alone. . . . The religion of Christ is not the tidbit after the bread; it is the bread itself, or it is nothing."[33]

This is at the heart of Bonhoeffer's "worldliness" that he commends to us. Instead of pitting the "real world" against the "spiritual world" and spawning conflict between the two, Bonhoeffer calls us to fully live in the world that is God's, and in our culture as God's disciple.

Culture is such a common word that we often use it loosely. The two extremes of either withdrawing from or conforming to the world tend to suffer from an anemic view of culture. The withdrawal approach has little if any space for a theology of creation, meaning not just our view of the origin of the earth, but our view of the current world as a place in which God is at work and his goodness is manifested. Theologians sometimes call the latter *common grace.* Those who wish to embrace culture uncritically do not distinguish between the good and the evil within it either. They neglect, in Bonhoeffer's words, the "fallen-falling" nature of the world.[34] Both approaches suffer from a lack of clear thinking on culture.

The clarity Bonhoeffer brings to the discussion concerns first distinguishing between creation and nature, or the creaturely and the natural.[35] The created world is the world before the fall. The natural world is the post-fallen world. He further distinguishes between the natural and the unnatural. The one who lives in the natural world understands the fall, even "accepts" it as the new reality in light of sin. The natural world too longs for redemption and reconciliation and ultimately re-creation in the new heav-

---

[32] Bonhoeffer, "Jesus Christ and the Essence of Christianity," December 11, 1928, *DBWE* 10:346.
[33] Ibid., 342.
[34] *DBWE* 3:120.
[35] *DBWE* 6:173ff.

ens and the new earth. The unnatural world is ultimately a false world, the world inhabited by those who naively pretend there is no God. Consequently, they falsely live as if there were no fall, no need of redemption, no need of reconciliation, and no coming of the new heavens and the new earth.

Bonhoeffer makes an interesting point, among many, when it comes to this natural view of the world: "In this context, there is good reason for the optimism about human history that persists within the limits of the fallen world."[36] This is a chastened optimism, a theologically astute optimism, if you will. It's also a source of hope, one that can instigate us to act in culture for human betterment. And, lest we forget, Bonhoeffer is writing this sentence from a prison cell in Nazi Germany.

For Bonhoeffer, it's true that the world is fallen-falling. To not understand the world and people accordingly is folly. It's also true, however, that the world is redeemed, that Christ has come and that the promises and covenants are initiated. And, keeping with his insight, we could add that the world is redeemed-redeeming, that is to say, God has begun the act of redemption and is moving the world to its full and final redemption.

This approach to culture and to discipleship is profoundly theological. Bonhoeffer stresses three doctrines in particular: creation, justification, and reconciliation. He further sees the eschatological dimension of these doctrines, pointing us to the ultimate reconciliation in the new heavens and the new earth. These three doctrines, and all of the teaching that they contain, explain how we can live "worldly" lives. Actually, in keeping with what we know of Bonhoeffer's theology, these three doctrines stem from one doctrine: christology. In Christ—his incarnation, his earthly life, his death, and his resurrection—we see what worldly living is truly like.

Into all this confusion over "being in the world but not of it," Dietrich Bonhoeffer offers clarity and sound direction, and he does so in his own compelling way. He first brings clarity by helping us think through a theology of culture and the world, a theology that takes into account the events of creation and the fall, of reconciliation in part ("the already"), and of reconciliation in full ("the not yet," or the new heavens and new earth to come). Bonhoeffer also brings clarity by focusing our attention on Christ. Ultimately, he looks to Christ for a definition of ethics. He looks to Christ for an understanding of genuine, full-blown worldliness. He looks to Christ to show us how to live the Christian life. This is why we can understand

---

[36] *DBWE* 6:177.

Bonhoeffer's view of discipleship as a christotelic discipleship. We follow Christ. And here's how.

Living Responsibly: The Four Mandates

For Bonhoeffer, culture as this "natural world," both fallen-falling and redeemed-redeeming, is our context. To see how God-given and Christ-driven (christotelic) culture is, Bonhoeffer understands culture as structured around what he terms the four mandates.

Early in *Ethics*, he observes, "The world stands in relationship to Christ whether the world knows it or not. This relation of the world to Christ becomes concrete in certain *mandates of God* in the world."[37] He then identifies four mandates as named in Scripture:

- work
- marriage
- government
- church

Bonhoeffer explains, "In the world God wills work, marriage, government, and church and God wills all of these, each in its own way, through Christ, toward Christ, and in Christ. . . . There can be no retreat, therefore, from a 'worldly' into a 'spiritual' realm."[38]

Work

When it comes to work, Bonhoeffer writes, "We encounter the mandate of Work in the Bible already with the first human being."[39] It is both a pre-fall and a post-fall mandate. "By the sweat of his brow Adam wrests nourishment from the field, and soon the range of human work embraces everything from agriculture through economic activity to science and art (Gen 4:17ff.)."[40] Bonhoeffer further refers to work as "cocreative human deeds," adding, "A world of things and values is created that is destined for the glory and service of Jesus Christ."[41] And "no one can withdraw from this mandate."[42]

Here is both a capacious and a redemptive view of work. While he was

---

[37] *DBWE* 6:68, emphasis his.
[38] *DBWE* 6:69.
[39] *DBWE* 6:70.
[40] *DBWE* 6:70.
[41] *DBWE* 6:70.
[42] *DBWE* 6:71.

in prison, he often asked for those outside to bring him books, sometimes specific titles, and he often discussed with his correspondents what he was reading. On one such occasion he mentions to his friend Eberhard, "It's a matter of great regret to me that I'm so ignorant of the natural sciences, but it's a gap that cannot be filled now."[43] He read and wrote of music, sociology, education and educational philosophy, and psychology. He saw these fields, and the contributions of those who worked within them, from this perspective of work as one of the four the mandates. He had a large view of God's world and what it means to glorify and serve him in it. It was for Eberhard's birthday in 1944 that Bonhoeffer wrote his poem "The Friend," which contains the lines,

> The work grows
> that gives a man's life
> substance and meaning.[44]

Bonhoeffer saw great value in work. I think it is part of the reason people find him so intriguing.

The testimonials of those who knew him while he was in prison speak of his discipline. He often referred to his work, whether he was keeping up with it or falling behind. That work was primarily with ideas and words. But he also valued physical labor. In a letter to Maria, Bonhoeffer shows us how the act of work can be redemptive. "Many people," he told her, "consider the most beneficial aspect of work to be its tendency to numb the psyche."[45] I've had a few of those mind-numbing jobs myself. But he counters, "Personally, I think what really matters is that the right kind of work renders one unselfish, and that a person whose heart is filled with personal interests and concerns develops a desire for such unselfishness in the service of others."[46] Working like this, as a means to cultivate unselfishness, is living a christotelic discipleship.

Marriage and the Home

Then there's the second mandate: marriage and the home. This too began with Adam and Eve, and this too is both a pre-fall and post-fall mandate.

---

[43] Bonhoeffer to Eberhard Bethge, February 2, 1944, *LPP*, 204.
[44] Bonhoeffer, "The Friend," August 28, 1944, *DBWE* 8:528.
[45] Bonhoeffer to Maria von Wedemeyer, August 13, 1944, in *Love Letters from Cell 92: The Correspondence between Dietrich Bonhoeffer and Maria von Wedemeyer, 1943–45*, ed. Ruth-Alice von Bismarck and Ulrich Kabitz, trans. John Brownjohn (Nashville: Abingdon, 1995), 260.
[46] Ibid.

Of the post-fall predicament, Bonhoeffer writes, "But because the first son of the first human beings, Cain, was born far from Paradise and became the murderer of his brother, here, too, a dark shadow falls over marriage and family in this our world."[47] Despite this dark shadow hovering over us, we are nevertheless called to live through, toward, and in Christ in our marriages and in our families. Bonhoeffer points out that Paul will come to refer to Christ's relationship to the church as a marriage (Eph. 5:1), not to mention that God is often referred to as our Father.[48] To live as christotelic disciples starts at home.

I am reminded of this negatively in the example of John Wesley. When his townhouse was built for him in London, on those rare occasions when he was actually in London, he made sure to have a private chamber built off the side of his bedroom to serve as his prayer closet. Yet, his legendary rocky marriage raged on while he retreated to his prayer closet for hours every morning.[49] There is something incompatible about this picture. Still, I hesitate to cite this example because of my own faults. And Wesley serves in so many ways as a model whom God used mightily.[50] The reality is that all of us can do better at loving our spouses and our children as Christ loves us and gave himself for us, and as God our heavenly Father loves us and gives us his good gifts.

Government

Next, Bonhoeffer considers the third mandate, government. Now he's venturing into difficult waters, given the context of his day. He starts with affirming the God-givenness of government, noting that government was given to establish justice and that "by establishing justice, and by the power of the sword, government preserves the world for the reality of Jesus Christ."[51] At this point in *Ethics*, this is all Bonhoeffer has to say. If we remember his letter to his prison interrogator, we realize that writing a political philosophy or a book on social ethics per se was not of interest to Bonhoeffer. His *polis* will come to be the church. He is not dodging the hard questions here or being cagey. He's after a distinctively "evangelical ethics." But that "evangelical ethics" of his throws us right back into the world.

---

[47] *DBWE* 6:71.
[48] *DBWE* 6:71.
[49] See Doreen Moore, *Good Christians, Good Husbands? Leaving a Legacy in Marriage and Ministry* (Ross-Shire, UK: Christian Focus, 2004).
[50] See Fred Sanders, *Wesley on the Christian Life: The Heart Renewed in Love* (Wheaton, IL: Crossway, 2013).
[51] *DBWE* 6:72–73.

Much later in *Ethics*, Bonhoeffer writes of the church's obligation to the world. But usually, he points out, we tend to go from the world to God. Instead, he calls us to go from God and his Word to the world. This is "the correct starting point."[52] He says: "The message of the church to the world can be none other than the word of God to the world. This word is: Jesus Christ and salvation in his name."[53] He elaborates, "The church's message to the world is the word about the coming of God in the flesh, about God's love for the world in the sending of God's son, about God's judgment on unbelief."[54] We will see in the next chapter how Bonhoeffer also sees the church as speaking Christ to the world in deeds as well as words, and we'll see the deeds Bonhoeffer himself engaged in as citizen. But for now, let his emphasis stand: "The church-community has to witness to the world concerning its faith in Christ."[55]

This emphasis is worth pausing over. Bonhoeffer is not here excluding civic engagement. Rather, he calls for us to have the right emphasis and order. We witness to the world first as the church witnesses to the Word. It is from this position that we then engage politics and social ethics. To put the matter another way, what the world needs most from the church is a solid witness to the Word, the gospel. That is the urgent call and task. But the world also needs our being good citizens. To put the matter even more directly: We are salt and light in the world primarily when we proclaim the gospel and also secondarily when we live and contend for virtue, right, and justice.

Church

The fourth mandate brings him to the church. This mandate concerns "eternal salvation" and is connected to the other three, yet also stands apart. It "reaches," as Bonhoeffer describes it, into the other three mandates. Bonhoeffer stresses this aspect of the mandate of the church because he wants us to see that

> Human Beings as whole persons stand before the whole earthly and eternal reality that God in Jesus Christ has prepared for them. . . . This is the witness the church has to give to the world, that all the other mandates

---

[52] *DBWE* 6:356.
[53] *DBWE* 6:356.
[54] *DBWE* 6:356.
[55] *DBWE* 6:357.

are not there to divide people and to tear them apart but to deal with them as whole people before God the Creator, Reconciler, and Redeemer—that reality in all its manifold aspects is ultimately one in God who became human, Jesus Christ.[56]

This is Bonhoeffer's *Christusleben*, the seeing of life—all of life—in Christ.[57]

Bonhoeffer, throughout his writings, offers insight into what it means to be the church, or the "church-community," as he comes to call it. But he makes many helpful observations in *Ethics*, among them this one: "The first task given to those who belong to the church is not to be something for themselves, for example, by creating a religious organization or leading a pious life, but to be witnesses of Jesus Christ to the world."[58] Later in *Ethics*, Bonhoeffer will speak of this as the church's obligation of proclamation; we are to see that "God's word is again and again spoken, pronounced, delivered, expounded, and spread."[59] This is Bonhoeffer remaining true to himself, always pushing us outward, always compelling us to look beyond ourselves, always calling us to the service of taking the gospel to and living the gospel before others.

Now we can come to appreciate Bonhoeffer's call to live worldly lives. He puts it forcefully:

> There is no real Christian existence outside the reality of the world and no real worldliness outside of the reality of Jesus Christ. For the Christian there is nowhere to retreat from the world, neither externally nor into the inner life. Every attempt to evade the world will have to be paid for sooner or later with a sinful surrender to the world.[60]

Bonhoeffer even adds an example: "It is a fact of experience that where the gross sins of sexuality are conquered, sins will flourish that are just as gross but less derided by the world, such as greed or avarice."[61] To understand this properly we need to see that he's not calling on us to take our discipleship any less seriously. On the contrary, we tend to take it far too casually. Merely keeping a few sins at bay is not discipleship. Discipleship is more than keeping our checklist of sins avoided and duties performed.

---

[56] *DBWE* 6:73.
[57] *DBWE* 6:58–61.
[58] *DBWE* 6:64.
[59] *DBWE* 6:396.
[60] *DBWE* 6:61.
[61] *DBWE* 6:61–62.

As Bonhoeffer would have us see it, *discipleship is living in all of our lives—in our work, in our marriages and families, in our citizenship, and in our church communities—through, toward, and in Christ.* Cheap imitations won't do.

Conclusion: Obeying the Commandments, Taking the Next Necessary Step

The four mandates of work, marriage, government, and church are the contexts for carrying out our lives toward, through, and in Christ—lives of radical worldliness. The commandments of Scripture provide the content. Bonhoeffer, however, goes further in seeing all of the commandments in Scripture as resting upon the foundation of the one concrete commandment, even declaring that the Ten Commandments and the Sermon on the Mount "are not two different ethical ideals, but *one* call to concrete obedience to the God and Father of Jesus Christ."[62] He goes one step further to see that Christ's call for us to love God and love our neighbor is this *one* commandment. Then he goes still a step further and sees this one commandment fulfilled in Christ himself. It's not only that Christ taught us to love God and others. Christ did love God and others. And, what's more, Christ is love. "*Christ* is the sole definition of love. . . . Love is always Jesus Christ himself."[63] This further reveals the contours of Bonhoeffer's christotelic discipleship. We obey Christ as we follow Christ in his world and in culture.

Whenever talk of the Christian and culture comes up, especially it seems among American evangelicals, the conversation soon turns to transforming culture. Too often, triumphalist views of transformation hold sway. These views tend to define the Christian's relationship to culture as a "culture war" and speak in terms of winning and losing. And more often than not, the winning and losing have to do with political means and political ends. Bonhoeffer offers a different model than triumphalism. His may be described as a cruciform model. We transform culture by living in light of Christ and proclaiming his name. There is a profound humility here that is sometimes absent in our culture-warrior stance.

Bonhoeffer also speaks a healthy word of caution to the transformation view when he reminds us that we are called not to change the world, but rather to take "the next necessary step." He writes:

---

[62] *DBWE* 6:359, emphasis his (in fact, the editors note that Bonhoeffer underlined the word "one" in this sentence two times).
[63] *DBWE* 6:335, emphasis his.

No one has the responsibility of turning the world into the kingdom of God, but only of taking the next necessary step that corresponds to God's becoming human in Christ. . . . The task is not to turn the world upside down but in a given place to do what, from the perspective of reality, is necessary objectively and to really carry it out. . . . It has to proceed step-by-step, ask what is possible, and entrust the ultimate step, and thus the ultimate responsibility, to another hand.[64]

It is encouraging to hear these words, which lift from our shoulders the weight of the world that we sometimes foolishly take on. We are only called to take the step that is in front of us.

A few paragraphs later, Bonhoeffer adds an even more encouraging note. He tells us pastorally that this kind of living "leaves human beings dependent on God's grace."[65]

It's comforting to remember that living the Christian life, discipleship, is maturing in Christ. The language of maturing reminds us that it is a process. We don't pop from salvation to instant maturity any more than we come into this world as mature adults. In that process of maturing we sometimes stumble, sometimes even fall. We don't always get right the balance of living "in the world but not of it." We don't always fully grasp the commands of God placed upon us as we work, as we live in our families, as we live as citizens in complex times, and as we live in the body of Christ. Not only do we find ourselves failing to fully grasp the commands, but we also at times fail to obey them. At that point God in his mercy and grace meets us. There are no heroes among us, not even our helpful and encouraging friend Bonhoeffer, who lays out this worldly, christotelic discipleship so nicely for us. We are all dependent upon God's grace to live as he's called us to live in the world he created, redeemed, and, in Christ, is reconciling to himself. To live in, through, and toward Christ is the essence of discipleship.

---

[64] *DBWE* 6:225.
[65] *DBWE* 6:227.

CHAPTER 8

FREEDOM

Today we in the church know far too little about the unique blessing of enduring and bearing—to bear, not to cast off, to bear, but neither to collapse, to bear as Christ bore the cross, to endure beneath it, and there, underneath, to find Christ.

**DIETRICH BONHOEFFER,
SERMON ON ROMANS 5:1–5, 1938**

Freedom's Just Another Word

In the fall of 1520, Luther was busy. He was excommunicated and he scribbled off his Three Treatises. He finished off the year with a bonfire, into which he threw the papal bull declaring him a heretic. One of those Three Treatises was *Freedom of the Christian Man*, or as it sometimes is called, *Christian Liberty*, in which he delivers his famous paradox:

> A Christian is a perfectly free lord of all, subject to none.
> A Christian is a perfectly dutiful servant of all, subject of all, subject to all.[1]

And so we have the challenge of defining freedom, or better, understanding what our freedom in Christ truly means. Kris Kristofferson, in what may well be the quintessential American song, "Me and Bobby McGee," shows his cynicism (or perhaps realism?) in the line that says, "Freedom's just another word for nothing left to lose." Philosophers, not

---

[1] Martin Luther, *The Three Treatises* (Minneapolis: Fortress, 1990), 277.

to mention politicians and even armies, have battled over the meaning of freedom for centuries.

It seems that the conversation about freedom is not far removed from that of happiness. Both of these may get at something far deeper still, what the Greeks referred to as the "good life" (*eudaimonia*). Again, a long succession of theories and books—not to mention bullets and wars—have sought after notions of the good life. Bonhoeffer, drawing on Luther's paradox, points us in the right direction. Of course, both Bonhoeffer and Luther draw on Christ's paradox of gaining one's life by losing it. So we come to the ultimate paradox: by service—and ultimately, by sacrifice—we are free, we are happy, we live the good life. True freedom is only freedom in Christ. True freedom, as Luther points out, is found in serving others. Bonhoeffer echoes that notion.

Peace in Pomerania

The Bible seems to go even deeper still than simply speaking of the good life. The biblical word is *shalom*: peace, rest, wholeness. Negatively, *shalom* is the absence of tension or anxiety, the utter removal of that nagging restlessness felt in the ever-waiting for the other shoe to drop. Our natural tendency, after Adam's dreadful fall, causes us to seek peace where it does not reside, either in ourselves or in our achievements. Of course, what we are speaking of here is our redemption. And redemption comes only in Christ and through his intercession—his humiliation, crucifixion, resurrection, and ascension.

Inge Karding, one of Bonhoeffer's students at Berlin, offers a chilling contrast: "Among the public there spread the expectation that the salvation of the German people would now come from Hitler. But in the lectures we were told that salvation comes only from Jesus Christ."[2]

Peace can seem elusive, whether the false prophet is a stirring politician turned megalomaniacal villain, as in the case of Adolf Hitler, or the false hope comes in a more subtle variety. But as we learn in one of the many seeming climaxes in the book of Romans, we have peace with God only through Jesus Christ (Rom. 5:1). Bonhoeffer preached on this exact text in 1938. Eberhard Bethge, who was with Bonhoeffer nearly every moment in those days, tells us that Bonhoeffer was writing *Life Together* in

---

[2] Inge Karding, in an interview with Martin Doblmeier, cited in Eric Metaxas, *Bonhoeffer: Pastor, Martyr, Prophet, Spy* (Nashville: Thomas Nelson, 2010), 119.

the recently vacated house of his twin sister and his Jewish brother-in-law. Bonhoeffer had arranged for them to flee Germany for London and, as it turned out, not a moment too soon. Bonhoeffer was also overseeing two collective pastorates, with around ten young ministers in training in each, in the back woods of Pomerania. The underground seminary had been shut down, and this was all that remained, like something out of Robin Hood and his merry men. At times, they even met in a hunting lodge. These small bands were the future of the Confessing Church. And Bonhoeffer preached to them on Romans 5 and what Paul has to say about peace in Christ. Before we look at the sermon, consider Paul's text:

> Therefore, since we have been justified by faith, we have peace with God through our Lord Jesus Christ. Through him we have also obtained access by faith into this grace in which we stand, and we rejoice in hope of the glory of God. Not only that, but we rejoice in our sufferings, knowing that suffering produces endurance, and endurance produces character, and character produces hope, and hope does not put us to shame, because God's love has been poured into our hearts through the Holy Spirit who has been given to us. (Rom. 5:1–5)

It's ironic that a text on peace tells us that we will suffer. This irony was not lost on Bonhoeffer, one who would have significant opportunity to suffer. When we think of what peace—or freedom, or happiness, or the good life, for that matter—entails, we tend not to include things like suffering and hardship, service and sacrifice, and even ultimately death. But these all made Bonhoeffer's list in a poem he entitled "Stations on the Road to Freedom."

Stations along the Way

On July 20, 1944, the "Valkyrie Plot" to kill Hitler in his field headquarters at Wolf's Lair failed. The bomb went off, destroying the room and taking the lives of a few of Hitler's inner circle. But Hitler himself escaped without harm, interpreting it as an act of Providence and using it to steel his nerve and press on with abandon in his murderous program. Hitler also unleashed his rage on the conspirators and the wider circle of the German Resistance, as just under five thousand were executed and a few thousand more were arrested directly as a result of the failed plot.

This all-out assault on the Resistance Movement eventually led to the discovery of the "Zossen" files in September 1944, the files kept by Hans von Dohnanyi, Dietrich's brother-in-law and high-ranking military intelligence officer. Dohnanyi kept these records as documentation of Hitler's war crimes and crimes against humanity for use after the war in bringing justice. The files also incriminated the conspirators in the previous plots.[3] Among these conspirators was the name of Dietrich Bonhoeffer. In October, Bonhoeffer was moved from Tegel to the cellar dungeon of the Gestapo headquarters at Prinz-Albrecht-Strasse in Berlin. His already long nightmare took a hellish turn. In February, Bonhoeffer would be moved to Buchenwald. In the early days of April, Bonhoeffer would be moved to Flossenbürg. And on April 9, 1945, Dietrich Bonhoeffer was hanged by the direct order of Hitler.[4] While Bonhoeffer was not involved in the Valkyrie Plot itself, it would be the unraveling of that very plot that would eventually lead him to the gallows.

Bonhoeffer heard the news of the failed plot on the "wireless" at Tegel on July 21, 1944. He knew the full weight and force of the implications of the failure. All he could do, as a prisoner already, was take up his pen. He wrote a letter to Bethge, as well as a poem, "Stations on the Road to Freedom." There are four stations: discipline, action, suffering, and finally death.

In a sense, these four stations represent Bonhoeffer's own maturing understanding of discipleship. The first represents his thinking in *The Cost of Discipleship*. In his letter to Bethge the day he wrote this poem, Bonhoeffer confessed, "I thought I could acquire faith by trying to live a holy life, or something like it. I suppose I wrote *The Cost of Discipleship* as the end of that path. Today I can see the dangers of that book, though I still stand by what I wrote."[5] He was not altogether dismissing his book. He was simply aware of the book's limitations, which reflect his own limitations at that time. The poem begins:

"Discipline"
If you set out to seek freedom, then learn above all things
to govern your soul and your senses, for fear that your passions

---

[3] The two failed assassination attempts in March 1943 led to the arrest of Bonhoeffer and others in April under suspicion. The files provided evidence against them, including Bonhoeffer.
[4] For a detailed discussion of this train of events, starting with the failure of the Valkyrie Plot and the eventual hanging of Bonhoeffer, see Eberhard Bethge, *Dietrich Bonhoeffer: A Biography*, enl. ed. (Minneapolis: Fortress, 2000), 893–941; and Metaxas, *Bonhoeffer*, 475–542. For a discussion of the ethical issues of Bonhoeffer's involvement in the conspiracies and a discussion of Bonhoeffer's death by execution or by martyrdom, see Craig J. Slane, *Bonhoeffer as Martyr: Social Responsibility and Modern Christian Commitment* (Grand Rapids: Brazos, 2004).
[5] Bonhoeffer to Eberhard Bethge, July 21, 1944, *LPP*, 369.

and longing may lead you away from the path that you should follow.
Chaste be your mind and your body, and both in subjection,
obediently, steadfastly seeking the aim set before them;
only through discipline may a man learn to be free.[6]

In this first stanza, the first station, we are introduced to the irony of freedom. Being free is not about being footloose and wanton. Being free is about being disciplined. By discipline, Bonhoeffer means living by the concrete command to love God and love others, to live according to God's commands. That obedience, steadfast obedience, is part of and flows from the life of faith. This echoes *The Cost of Discipleship*, though here Bonhoeffer has more in mind our preparedness, our character, our interior self that is brought into check. But for him, this station is not the end. There's something more.

The disciplined life leads to the next station, that of "Action."

"Action"
Daring to do what is right, not what fancy may tell you,
valiantly grasping occasions, not cravenly doubting—
freedom comes only through deeds, not through thoughts taking wing.
Faint not nor fear, but go out to the storm and the action,
trusting in God whose commandment you faithfully follow;
freedom, exultant, will welcome your spirit with joy.[7]

Here he advocates a bold living, again flowing from faith and trust in God. Bonhoeffer commends the countercultural life, the life that requires valiant action, not in the comfortable times, but in the "storm" of life. Don't miss, either, that Bonhoeffer introduces the idea of joy at this point. His move here, as with all of the poem, is counterintuitive. Joy comes through hardship and commitment. But again, this isn't the end for Bonhoeffer. Here, too, we hear the echoes of *The Cost of Discipleship*.

Bonhoeffer titles the third station "Suffering." Here again we see the counterintuitive move as he declares suffering to be good for us. A few days after composing this poem, he wrote in yet another letter to Bethge, "Suffering is a way to freedom. In suffering, the deliverance consists in our being allowed to put the matter out of our own hands into God's hands."[8]

---

[6] Bonhoeffer, "Stations on the Road to Freedom," July 21, 1944, *LPP*, 370–71.
[7] Ibid., 371.
[8] Bonhoeffer to Eberhard Bethge, July 25, 1944, *LPP*, 375.

Bonhoeffer addressed suffering in *The Cost of Discipleship*, but not quite like this. We're starting to see the something more he's learned in the intervening time since he wrote his classic text.

Suffering is good for us because it drives us to God. Suffering brings to the surface our frailty and weakness. And as we saw in chapter 2 and the discussion of Bonhoeffer's preaching of 2 Corinthians 12 in London, God displays his strength in our weakness. So here Bonhoeffer explains:

> "Suffering"
> A change has come indeed. Your hands, so strong and active,
> are bound;[9] in helplessness now you see your action
> is ended; you sigh in relief, your cause committing[10]
> to stronger hands; so now you may rest contented.
> Only for one blissful moment could you draw near to touch freedom;
> then it might be preferred in glory, you gave it to God.[11]

While ostensibly about the plots against Hitler, this stanza throws a wide enough net to encompass the times in our life when we suffer and do not see the desired result, times when (as the psalmist bemoans) the righteous suffer and the wicked prosper. This is about living in life's perplexities. If we go back to the letter to Bethge, we read, "It is only by living completely in the world that one learns to have faith. . . . By this-worldliness I mean living unreservedly in life's duties, problems, successes and failures, experiences and perplexities."[12] By living this way, "We throw ourselves completely into the arms of God." Moreover, in doing so we take seriously not only "our own sufferings, but those of God in the world—watching with Christ in Gethsemane."[13]

Here, too, we see the wide gulf between the costly discipleship Bonhoeffer commends and the cheap grace he castigates in *The Cost of Discipleship*. In that book, Bonhoeffer reminds us that discipleship means conforming to the image of Christ, which entails suffering. "It is the image of one who places himself in the very midst of the world of sin and death . . . who remains obedient to God's will in suffering and death . . . and who, on

---

[9] This is Bonhoeffer's expression of his inability to do anything while imprisoned. He knew of the Valkyrie Plot, but, being in prison, could not do anything for it.

[10] Bonhoeffer here is referencing the Valkyrie Plot, as well as the plots he had been involved in.

[11] Again with reference to the plots, Bonhoeffer here expresses that moment of hope as the plots were carried out that they would be successful. "Stations on the Road to Freedom," July 21, 1944, *LPP*, 371.

[12] Bonhoeffer to Eberhard Bethge, July 21, 1944, *LPP*, 369–70.

[13] Ibid., 370.

the cross, was rejected and abandoned by God and human beings."[14] Then Bonhoeffer adds that those same wounds "have now become the signs of grace."[15] Bonhoeffer embraces suffering—the life of perplexity and failure and shortcomings and disappointed hopes—not because he's an incurable pessimist or an ascetic, but because suffering drives him to grace.

The final station is perhaps the most counterintuitive point Bonhoeffer has to make. His last words before he was hanged were, "This is for me the end, the beginning of life." So he views death as our ultimate freedom. This is a powerful belief in the resurrection. The resurrection and our union with the triune God are the end of the life lived in, through, and toward Christ. This is not a death wish. Bonhoeffer ends his letter to Bethge, "Keep well, and don't lose hope that we shall all meet again soon."[16] Still, his final stanza declares full faith in God by knowing that we will be with God in eternity:

> "Death"
> Come now, thou greatest of fests on the journey to freedom eternal;
> death, cast aside all burdensome chains, and demolish
> the walls of our temporal body, the walls of our souls that are blinded,
> so that at last we may see that which here remains hidden.
> Freedom, how long we have sought thee in discipline, action, and
>   suffering;
> dying, we now may behold thee revealed in the Lord.[17]

As John writes, "Beloved, we are God's children now, and what we will be has not yet appeared; but we know that when he appears we shall be like him, because we shall see him as he is" (1 John 3:2). Paul says similarly that someday this "light momentary affliction" will give way to "an eternal weight of glory beyond all comparison" (2 Cor. 4:17; cf. 3:12–5:5).

Bonhoeffer appended a note to the poem, apologizing for the "unpolished" and "rough" nature of it, and adding, "I'm certainly no poet!"[18] Usually Bonhoeffer has good judgment, but here he's wide of the mark. He's not only a remarkable poet; he's a remarkable theologian. In this poem and in the letter, Bonhoeffer shows how so much of our preconceptions about freedom, happiness, and peace—the quest for living the good life—are in

---

[14] *DBWE* 4:284.
[15] *DBWE* 4:284.
[16] Bonhoeffer to Eberhard Bethge, July 21, 1944, *LPP*, 370.
[17] Bonhoeffer, "Stations on the Road to Freedom," July 21, 1944, *LPP*, 371.
[18] Bonhoeffer to Eberhard Bethge, July 21, 1944, "Accompanying Note," *LPP*, 372.

fact misconceptions. He points us in a different direction. This direction starts with discipline and action, out of faith in and obedience to God. But it also embraces suffering because suffering propels us to Christ and to his marvelous grace. And finally, Bonhoeffer leads us in a direction that does not see death as the end or as the final curtain brought down on our achievements and quests, but, again in faith and looking to Christ, sees death as the beginning of our promised inheritance of eternal life in Christ.

This poem, "Stations on the Road to Freedom," echoes the Christ-centered or christotelic emphasis we have come to see in so much of Bonhoeffer's writings. In Christ's humiliation we see discipline, action, suffering, and ultimately death. In Christ's crucifixion we see all four as well. And in Christ's resurrection we see his triumph over death and over suffering. In the risen and living Christ we see the triumph of freedom.

To make these stations, and living in light of them, a bit more concrete in our lives, we need to explore more deeply Bonhoeffer's understanding of happiness and contentment in service and sacrifice. In our day, this is all the more important. A few decades ago sociologists spoke of our incessant self-preoccupation in modern times.[19] Since then, self-obsession has seemed only to proliferate like so many Facebook pages or YouTube videos. As fallen human beings we've been perennially plagued by narcissism, but it's hard to avoid the ubiquity of it today. Being in Christ does not make us immune to such selfish and inward pulls. We too need to learn deference to the other, love for our neighbor, and selfless service. Being so self-absorbed, we may have lost the virtue of sacrifice.

Sacrifice: (Also Known as) Contentment

Puritan minister Jeremiah Burroughs wrote a book entitled *The Rare Jewel of Christian Contentment*. Contentment is rare, of course, because it so often eludes us. Bonhoeffer helps us find it. Going back to his sermon in Pomerania on Romans 5:1–5, he speaks of the afflictions and hardships that have come upon the Confessing Church. He even says, "Nobody knows what afflictions still lie ahead for the church."[20] He speaks of how these afflictions should come as no surprise. Throughout the New Testament, followers of Christ are called to suffer. Paul's teaching in Romans 5 is no exception.

---

[19] David Wells wrote of this perceptively in *No Place for Truth: Or, Whatever Happened to Evangelical Theology* (Grand Rapids: Eerdmans, 1994).
[20] Bonhoeffer, sermon on Rom. 5:1–5, September 3, 1938, *DBWE* 15:474.

In fact, Paul calls on us to "rejoice in our sufferings" (5:2–3). That joy, Bonhoeffer points out, comes in bearing under the load of service, enduring with one another and bearing with one another. Bonhoeffer sees the joy in what suffering produces. It produces patience (or endurance), which produces character, which produces hope. Additionally, we rejoice because "God's love has been poured into us" (5:5). "The gate of sorrow, of loss, of dying shall become for us the gate of the great hope in God, the gate of honor and glory."[21] That's cause for joy.

Not everyone sees suffering this way. In fact Bonhoeffer refers back to Luther's observation that for some, "affliction produces impatience, impatience produces hardness of heart, hardness of heart leads to despair, and despair brings ruin."[22] Too often that's how we see affliction and hardship. Sadly, more often than not it only takes small afflictions to cause us to falter. And then we head off the rails. Our derailment occurs, Bonhoeffer says, when "we prefer an earthly peace with the world to the peace with God, if we love the securities of our life more than God. Then affliction will turn into our ruin."[23]

Cultivating this view of enduring affliction and practicing patience does not come easily. Bonhoeffer writes, "In the church today, we know much too little about the strange blessing of bearing something. Bearing, but not shaking it off, bearing, but also not collapsing underneath."[24] How do we not collapse? Bonhoeffer answers, "Bearing as Christ bore the cross, remaining below, and there below—finding Christ."[25]

Bonhoeffer writes similarly in *The Cost of Discipleship*. Here he is thinking of Mark 8:31–38, as well as Matthew 11:28–30 and Christ's call to discipleship. Bonhoeffer notes, "Discipleship is being bound to the suffering Christ. That is why Christian suffering is not disconcerting. Instead, it is nothing but grace and joy."[26] Christ bears us up as we bear up and bear one another. There is no place we should rather be than under the cross of Christ.

If patience comes in suffering and "bearing," and joy comes in suffering and "bearing," then we have stumbled upon a rather counterintuitive and countercultural way to live. But it is one that can save us from spoiling so much of our lives wallowing in disappointment and grumbling in

---

[21] Ibid., 475.
[22] Ibid., 476.
[23] Ibid.
[24] Ibid.
[25] Ibid.
[26] *DBWE* 4:89.

circumstances. In a 1942 letter to his twin sister, Sabine, and her husband, Gerhard Leibholz, then living in London, Bonhoeffer writes of the news of Sabine's daughter's confirmation. Bonhoeffer was the godfather *in absentia*. He expresses how "important [it is] that she finds her way to Christianity and the church." He adds:

> There are so many experiences and disappointments which make a way for nihilism and resignation for sensitive people. So it is good to learn early enough that suffering and God is not a contradiction but rather a necessary unity; for me the idea that God himself is suffering has always been one of the most convincing teachings of Christianity. I think God is nearer to suffering than to happiness and to find God in this way gives peace and rest and a strong and courageous heart.[27]

Bonhoeffer addresses this issue of disappointment and contentment in one of his last letters from Tegel. Writing to Bethge, he observes, "God does not give us everything we want, but he does fulfill all his promises"; he adds that God graciously is "constantly renewing our faith and not laying on us more than we can bear, gladdening us with his nearness and help, hearing our prayers, and leading us along the straightest and best paths to himself."[28] In short, God is faithful, and he's faithful to us ultimately because of Christ and our secure place in him.

Bonhoeffer could even resign his anxieties and frustrations and anger toward Hitler and his machinations by taking comfort in God's control and faithfulness. In a poem "The Death of Moses," Bonhoeffer moves from the difficulties in the exodus and the wilderness wanderings to the promises and fulfillment bound up in the Holy Land. The poem also moves from the past, and the history of Israel, to the present. This is quite clear in the lines,

> God's own justice guards both weak and strong
> from the whim of tyranny and wrong.[29]

The tyrant, Hitler, was not outside God's control and would indeed some-day face God's judgment. Bonhoeffer took comfort in this. He ends the poem longing for the peace and blessing that reign in the Promised Land.

---

[27] Bonhoeffer to the Leibholz family, May 21, 1942, *DBWE* 16:284.
[28] Bonhoeffer to Eberhard Bethge, August 14, 1944, *LPP*, 387.
[29] Bonhoeffer, "The Death of Moses," *DBWE* 8:537. The editors note that "wrong" is not the best translation, but it is used only to capture the rhyme of Bonhoeffer's German in the translation to English. The German word Bonhoeffer used, *Gewalt*, is better translated as "violence."

"Underneath the cross," Bonhoeffer reminds us in his Romans sermon, "there is peace.... Here is the only way in the world to find peace with God. God's wrath is stilled in Jesus Christ alone.... Therefore, for the church-community of Christ, his cross becomes the eternal source of joy and hope in the coming glory of God."[30]

Bonhoeffer's emphasis on the church-community should not be missed. We bear with one another. He, of course, has a great deal to say about this in *Life Together*, as we saw in chapter 3 above. One sentence from a poem at Tegel, though, captures the beauty of our intercession for one another in and through suffering:

> Brother, till the night be past,
> Pray for me![31]

Neither should we miss the christotelic discipleship Bonhoeffer calls us to live. This was no "war-time urgency" for Bonhoeffer. Even back in his New Year's sermon preached while in London in 1934, Bonhoeffer was proclaiming this message of the Christian life as following Christ. He closed that particular sermon by also pointing his congregation to Christ: "The coming year will have its share of fear, guilt, and hardship. But let it be, in all our fear, guilt, and hardship, a year spent with Christ. Let our new beginning with Christ be followed by a story of going with Christ. What that means is beginning each day with him. That is what matters."[32] This is how we ultimately find the rare jewel of contentment—of the good life, of happiness, and of peace—by starting, going, and someday ending with Christ.

Conclusion: Speak Weakness to Power

In the galleries of the Philadelphia Museum of Art hangs a painting by the Italian artist Pacecco de Rosa entitled "The Massacre of the Innocents" (c. 1640). Quite large, measuring over six by ten feet, the painting stuns viewers otherwise walking casually by. There are three groups in the painting. There are soldiers, Herod's soldiers, with faces twisted in violent rage and sheer hatred. There are mothers, faces in anguish, arms outstretched, vainly attempting to keep the soldiers' spears from

---

[30] Bonhoeffer, sermon on Rom. 5:1–5, September 3, 1938, *DBWE* 15:472–73.
[31] Bonhoeffer, "Night Voices in Tegel," July 1944, *LPP*, 355.
[32] Bonhoeffer, meditation on Luke 9:57–62, January 1, 1934, *DBWE* 13:349.

their children. And then there are the children, infants. The painting well depicts the horror of this event recorded in Scripture, recalling Herod's attempt to do away with one child, the Christ, by eliminating all males under two years of age. And the cries of Rachel weeping went up across the land (Matt. 2:16–18).

Bonhoeffer preached on this passage in 1939, again, to the collective pastorate. He says, "Even if a murderous Herod puts his cruel hands in play, in the end everything will go as God has seen, intends, and spoken."[33] The application would be rather obvious to all in the room. *Kristallnacht* had just occurred one month earlier, in November. That was, sadly, only the beginning as Hitler would soon embark on his own gruesome slaughter that would rage on until the end of April 1945.

Bonhoeffer returns to those infants who fell under the soldier's spears: "They become the first martyrs of Christendom, the dying witnesses for the life of Christ, their savior."[34] Then he references the cry of Rachel, noting:

> The lament for the martyrs of Jesus Christ begins, and it will not quiet down until the end of time. It is the lament for the world estranged from God and an enemy of Christ, for the blood of the innocents, for our own guilt and sin for which Christ himself experienced suffering. But with this inconsolable lamentation, there is one great consolation: Jesus Christ lives, and we will live with him if we suffer with him.[35]

Even this horrible act, "as ungodly and as gruesome as it was, nevertheless had to serve God, who brings his promises to fulfillment. Sorrow and tears come upon God's people, but they are precious to God, for they are offerings for Christ's sake, and Christ will take them up in eternity."[36]

Bonhoeffer here is not merely sentimentalizing suffering, nor is he whitewashing the problem of evil and the sufferer's question, where is God in all of this? Rather, he's tackling it head-on. What we see in suffering and sacrifice is not an easy answer, nor do we see a sophisticated philosophical one. Instead we see the cross and we see Christ.[37] On another occasion Bonhoeffer said, "War, sickness, and hunger must come, so that the gospel of the kingdom of peace, of love, and of salvation can be spoken and heard

---

[33] Bonhoeffer, sermon on Matt. 2:13–23, December 31, 1940, *DBWE* 15:491.
[34] Ibid., 493.
[35] Ibid.
[36] Ibid.
[37] For more on this theologically rich answer to the philosophical problem of evil, see Henri Blocher, *Evil and the Cross: An Analytical Look at the Problem of Pain* (Grand Rapids: Kregel, 2005).

all the more keenly, all the more clearly, all the more deeply. . . . War serves peace, hate serves love, the devil serves God, the cross serves life."[38]

It's difficult to speak truth to power. In the face of power, one often turns the coward and folds. But if it takes courage to speak truth to power, it takes more courage to change the rules of the game, to speak weakness to power. When we turn and face God, we meet him in weakness on the cross. That is what Bonhoeffer was attempting to convey to these young ministers-to-be, early-twenty-somethings, who were about to be thrust into service in the church in Germany's darkest hour. Bonhoeffer was smart enough to know that difficult and hard and cruel times were coming. And to answer those perplexing and challenging moments, he pointed them to Christ, who came "to share the life of those who are disregarded and despised, so that he may bear the misery of all human beings and become their savior."[39] And he called them to preach Christ and him crucified—to speak weakness, to speak Christ—to power.

In his sermon on Romans 5:1–5, Bonhoeffer references the hymn they sang as part of the service. The first line runs, "The day is over: my Jesus, stay with me."[40] In 1938, Bonhoeffer was already acutely aware of hardship, but soon he would be entering the long, dark night himself.

Bonhoeffer would also in the next few years engage in plots to put an end to Germany's long night by cutting off the head of the snake. Much has been written of Bonhoeffer and the legitimacy or illegitimacy of his role as a spy in the military intelligence, the *Abwehr*, which was quite overrun with Resistance Movement figures, including the officer Bonhoeffer directly reported to, Hans Oster. Eric Metaxas notes how the idea that Bonhoeffer join the *Abwehr* sprang from his brother-in-law Hans von Dohnanyi, already a member. Bonhoeffer had been under watch and harassed by the Gestapo for several years. By being a member of the *Abwehr*, Dohnanyi reasoned, Bonhoeffer would be left alone by the Gestapo and could carry on his work in the Confessing Church, especially that of visiting young ministers and continuing to train them unimpeded. With his *Abwehr* papers, Bonhoeffer could travel freely.[41]

Dohnanyi, Oster, and the head of the *Abwehr*, Admiral Canaris, were all involved in the conspiracy against Hitler, first in attempting a military coup.

---

[38] Dietrich Bonhoeffer, "National Memorial Day Sermon," in *The Collected Sermons of Dietrich Bonhoeffer*, ed. Isabel Best (Minneapolis: Fortress, 2012), 20–21.

[39] Bonhoeffer, sermon on Matt. 2:13–23, December 31, 1940, *DBWE* 15:494.

[40] Bonhoeffer, sermon on Rom. 5:1–5, September 3, 1938, *DBWE* 15:472n3.

[41] Metaxas, *Bonhoeffer*, 369ff.

They used Bonhoeffer and his connections to get messages to British contacts to elicit support. These *Abwehr* officers had Bonhoeffer travel "to carry preliminary information about the planned coup to [Bonhoeffer's] foreign contacts."[42] When plans for the coup failed, the conspirators continued in their efforts to assassinate Hitler. The planning was carried out by these officers. Bonhoeffer was far more engaged with his church work and writing—despite the Gestapo's having formally banned him from writing. During this period, 1941 through 1943, Bonhoeffer also supplied information regarding persecution of Jews, especially "collecting data" during the Order of Deportation in September 1941.[43] This data contributed to reports of the situation that went to key military officers, Resistance Movement members all.[44]

That seems to be the extent of Bonhoeffer's conspiratorial involvement. He was certainly not a military type, planning or carrying out the assassination attempts. In the wake of the Valkyrie Plot, yet another failed attempt on Hitler's life, Dohnanyi, Oster, Canaris, and Bonhoeffer were all moved to the Gestapo prison in Berlin. All four were hanged together on April 9, 1945, at Flossenbürg Concentration Camp.

In my view, the involvement in the conspiracy is part of his long run of resistance to Hitler, starting back with Bonhoeffer's calling Hitler a *Dis-Fuhrer* (misleader) in 1932. It includes his work in helping Jews flee Germany by his many contacts throughout Europe and in Great Britain. He did not enter into the conspiracies lightly. In fact, he wondered whether by doing so he was damning his own soul. But he saw no other choice. I find it hard to judge Bonhoeffer on this score, having never experienced anything like what he experienced or been in a context anywhere near as difficult. Philosophers debate ethical dilemmas in the cool environs of the classroom (or on the blogosphere). But Bonhoeffer lived right in the center of history's most intense ethical dilemma.

While I find it hard to judge him for whatever role he played in the conspiracies, I find it not so hard to call him a martyr. In July 1988, ten statues were unveiled on the west front of Westminster Abbey in London. With parts of the Cathedral dating to the Middle Ages, Westminster has been long in the making. This recent addition of statues commemorates the martyrdoms of the twentieth century as represented in ten figures. Among

---

[42] Bethge, *Dietrich Bonhoeffer*, 724.
[43] Bethge records, "Bonhoeffer collected all the facts he could confirm, to pass them on to sympathizers in the army command," ibid., 745.
[44] See ibid., 722–80, for the full discussion of Bonhoeffer as spy; see also Metaxas, *Bonhoeffer*, 369–431.

them is the Lutheran pastor Dietrich Bonhoeffer. I think he rightfully takes his place as a martyr. If there ever was a personification of evil on earth it was Hitler. Bonhoeffer withstood him, not because of some mere nationalism in the patriotic service of the true Germany, but because Bonhoeffer saw the pure evil that Hitler was. Bonhoeffer felt compelled to act, and for that, Hitler put him to death. Bonhoeffer once spoke of the need, at times, to be a "spoke in the wheel."[45] It's not enough, he realized, simply to bandage up those crushed under the wheel; sometimes the need is to stop the wheel. That's how he saw it. And whether he was right or wrong will quite likely be the source of debate for years to come.

However one interprets Bonhoeffer and this act—his final act of sacrifice—we know one thing for certain: Bonhoeffer's death would not be the last word. That place belongs to love.

---

[45] Cited in Metaxas, *Bonhoeffer,* 154.

CHAPTER 9

LOVE

*May God give [faith] to us daily. And I do not mean the faith which
flees the world, but the one that endures the world and which loves and
remains true to the world in spite of all the suffering which it contains
for us. Our marriage shall be a yes to God's earth; it shall strengthen
our courage to act and accomplish something on the earth. I fear that
Christians who stand with only one leg upon earth also stand with only
one leg in heaven.*

**DIETRICH BONHOEFFER
TO HIS FIANCÉE, MARIA VON WEDEMEYER,
FROM TEGEL PRISON, 1943**

*A King who dies on the cross must be the King of a rather strange
kingdom.*

DIETRICH BONHOEFFER, 1928

Somewhere near the top of the list of our problems and challenges in the
twenty-first century has to be our penchant for the trivial. Culture watchers
such as Neil Postman and theologians such as David Wells have sounded
the alarm of our incessant need and our stunning ability to trivialize. Postman chalks it up to our entertainment and amusement culture—a culture
that inundates us with images. Consider this. We can sit and watch a com-
mercial for Compassion International, being confronted with images of
malnourished and deprived children halfway around the world. Then that

image is immediately followed up with bikini-clad beach-volleyball play-
ers in the service of selling us on all the promises bound up in a bottle of
light beer. It's not merely the juxtaposition of images here. This incessant
pounding of images takes its toll. We are left numb to anything of substance and significance. We don't seem to even notice or tend to care about
the deep problems or issues around us. We're lost in the juxtaposition of
images. We ooh and aah at the trivial.

In our drowning in the sea of the trivial, we have lost the meaning of
things, the meaning of people, even the meaning of life. Bonhoeffer, in his
own day, could see this. He writes, "For many today man is just a part of
the world of things, because the experience of the human simply eludes
them."[1] This lack of meaningful experiences is stronger, I would propose,
in our ever-increasing virtual world.

This lack of meaningful experiences also leads us to lose the significance of words, the vocabulary we use to give expression to those experiences. Once we deflate words of their power and substance, we weaken the
connections we have to the world. So we have a strange irony in our day.
We know acutely of the deprived child halfway around the globe—far more
acutely, in fact, than we could have in previous ages. But we are left nearly
powerless to feel and to respond substantively.

The Extraordinary

This problem of trivialization manifests itself in various ways. We are so
inundated with images, we have become numb. We are so flippant in our
language, we have become unable to communicate meaningfully. We are
so caught up in what we are told to think, to do, and to buy, we have become
unable to reflect, analyze, or criticize. And maybe worse, we have been so
dehumanized that we have become unable to love. We lust heartily after
images, shadows. We have come to cherish cheap substitutes. We have lost
the meaning and the significance of love.

As we have seen, Bonhoeffer gives much of the space in *The Cost of
Discipleship* to a discourse on the Sermon on the Mount. Now we see why
Bonhoeffer's book is so challenging, as its backbone is one of the most challenging texts we come across in the New Testament. Just when we think
we know what love is, after coming to Christ and reading God's Word—
that we are to love God and neighbor—then Christ comes along with the

---

[1] Bonhoeffer to Eberhard Bethge, August 14, 1944, *LPP*, 386.

command to "love your enemies" (Matt. 5:44). Bonhoeffer calls this "the Extraordinary."[2] And this he sees as the dividing line between cheap imitations of discipleship and the real thing.

Bonhoeffer is intrigued by the placement of this command from Christ to love our enemies. He sees it as shining a light back on the Beatitudes, explaining what it means to be salt and a city, prominently displaying its light upon a hill. And what's most important of all, Bonhoeffer sees how Christ himself fulfills his own command to love our enemies in his death on the cross for sinners, the enemies of God (Rom. 5:8–10). "What is the extraordinary?" he asks. "It is the love of Jesus Christ himself, who goes to the cross in suffering and obedience. It is the cross. What is unique to Christianity is the cross, which allows Christians to step beyond the world in order to receive victory over the world."[3]

The ethics of the Sermon on the Mount are nothing less than extraordinary. To look at them as something that can be fulfilled within the ordinary and by ordinary means is foolish. Bonhoeffer writes that loving one's enemies "demands more than the strength a natural person can muster."[4] Only from the perspective of the cross do the ethics of the Sermon on the Mount become possible; only by living from the cross can the ethical demands of Jesus come to pass in our lives. Again, "In Christ the crucified and his community, the 'extraordinary' occurs."[5] Do we really understand what love is? Or, to put the matter another way, who among us truly understands being a follower of Christ, a disciple? If left on our own, we would not get very far in answering these questions. So we see in Christ and we find in Christ what we need. But Bonhoeffer still calls *us* to live this way, not simply calling us to see *Christ* living this way.

"The extraordinary is doubtless that which is visible, which magnifies the Father in heaven," Bonhoeffer declares. "It cannot remain hidden. The people have to see it."[6] And so we live out of love for God, for our neighbor, and for our enemy. That kind of life by definition does not conform to the world. It radically transforms it. Bonhoeffer ends his discussion on the Sermon on the Mount by acknowledging that various interpretations of this text abound. Simultaneously, he asserts, "Jesus knows only one possibility:

---

[2] The editors of *DBWE* 4 note that Bonhoeffer uses this word to get at the Greek word from Matt. 5:47, *perisson*. Bonhoeffer uses Luther's translation, which has the German word *Sonderliches*, "something strange." *DBWE* 4:144n153.
[3] *DBWE* 4:144.
[4] *DBWE* 4:138.
[5] *DBWE* 4:145.
[6] *DBWE* 4:145.

simply go and obey."[7] "Jesus has spoken," Bonhoeffer observes. "Our part is to obey."[8] Now we can be thankful for God who supplies the grace to obey, to go and love as Christ loved.

Here we are moving out of the sandbox, as it were. There's a way we can play at church or play at being a Christian that doesn't measure up to the standard set in the Sermon on the Mount. There is also a way we can twist this into a legalism. We can be quite skillful at moralizing. We can be even better at self-righteousness. So we must flip back to the early pages of Bonhoeffer's *Cost of Discipleship* to see how quickly he takes us to grace. He says much the same thing in a paper he had written in 1930 while in America: "Only the Christian conception of grace makes man before God free and gives so the only possible basis for ethical life."[9] One page earlier, Bonhoeffer states, "Man lives in faith of his justification and sanctification; he can never say: I am good, he always must say: 'forgive my debts' and he must believe in his justification. . . . Grace is made the only and new foundation of human life."[10] Grace pulses through *The Cost of Discipleship* as well.

I find it interesting that he begins *The Cost of Discipleship* by talking about cheap grace and costly grace—on the very first page, in the very first sentence. He could just as easily have started with cheap discipleship and costly discipleship. But he started as he did, I think, to remind us of grace. He knew what was coming in the following chapters. He knew he would be spending significant time commending Christ's commands from Matthew 5–7, as well as the hard commands elsewhere in Scripture. He knew we need to remember that we live by grace. And we need to remember that we can bring all of God's commands down to one: to love.

It was Augustine who said, or maybe it was Luther, as both are cited as the source, "Love God and do as you please." This is not license, but a call to the highest ethic. While Bonhoeffer does not get counted among those credited for the quote, he easily could have been the one to coin it. And so I offer this succinct synopsis of Bonhoeffer on the Christian life: We live in love by grace as the church-community—in, through, and toward Christ.

For all that Bonhoeffer has to teach us on discipleship, this is the distillation and essence of it. As we come to this topic of love, we come to the summit of Bonhoeffer's teaching on the Christian life. Everything in the prior chapters has been leading us up to this point.

---

[7] *DBWE* 4:181.
[8] *DBWE* 4:182.
[9] *DBWE* 10:451.
[10] *DBWE* 10:450.

Our look at his christology (chap. 2) and ecclesiology (chap. 3) laid the foundation for it. Our discussion of Scripture and reading and living God's Word (chap. 4), our discussion of prayer (chap. 5), and our discussion of thinking and living theologically (chap. 6) all explained the particular means by which we learn and practice it. Our most recent discussions of being "worldly" (chap. 7) and of freedom and service and sacrifice (chap. 8) were looking at manifestations of it. Now, what remains is to travel to the peak itself, to see Bonhoeffer's views on love and his life of love. We begin at home.

Love Letters

We see Bonhoeffer's care for his family members most poignantly in his letters during his imprisonment. Themes quickly emerge. One theme is how readily he offers reassurances to his family of his well-being. He hopes they do not suffer anguish over him and his imprisonment and whatever outcome awaits him. His hope for them concerns their peace, their rest. When he hears of a family member's illness or sad circumstance—indirectly, for his family too refrained from expressing their troubles to him—he instantly writes. He quickly offers encouragement.

On December 28, 1944, from his dungeon cell in Berlin, he somehow manages to score the privilege of writing his mother a letter for her birthday. He writes, "All I really want to do is to help cheer you a little in these days that you must be finding so bleak. Dear mother, I want you to know that I am constantly thinking of you and father every day, and that I thank God for all that you are to me and to the whole family."[11]

This is no isolated letter. Nor is this concern for the other, his neighbor, isolated to his family. We'll see below Bonhoeffer's concern for others expressed in deeds of love. But there remains one relationship of his worthy of discussion. In January 1943, Dietrich Bonhoeffer became engaged to Maria von Wedemeyer. She had written him on January 13 saying yes to his proposal, which he expressed in a letter. He received her letter on January 17, a Sunday. If he was a strict Sabbath-keeper, he broke it. Merely sixty minutes later he was writing her back:

> I thank you for your word [of yes], for all you have endured for me and for what you are and will be for me. Let us now be and become happy in each

[11] Bonhoeffer to his mother, December 28, 1944, *LPP* 399.

other. . . . Let us encounter each other in great free forgiveness and love. Let us take each other as we are—with thanks and boundless trust in God, who has led us to this point and loves us.[12]

It's fitting that their engagement would officially begin in letters, for after his arrest on April 5, 1943, their relationship would consist mostly of correspondence, except for far too few but extremely cherished visits in prison. Of their relationship consisting mostly of love letters, Bethge would later say, "We are thus confronted by written testimony to a remarkable engagement and a love story rich in self-denial."[13] Jürgen Moltmann, who as a rather reluctant soldier in the German army "surrendered" to the first British soldier he saw and later became one of Germany's leading theologians, would call the relationship "a deeply moving love story in a deadly time."[14]

As with the rest of Bonhoeffer's letters, themes quickly emerge. Hope, thankfulness, and trust pepper these letters. These virtues can be difficult to cultivate in the best of times and circumstances. Dietrich and Maria cultivated them together while she was dodging air raids and he sat in prison. Writing from his cell, Bonhoeffer anticipates their first Christmas as an engaged couple: "Let us approach Christmas-tide not only undaunted but with complete confidence. And should God's mercy reunite us we shall have the finest earthly Christmas gifts in each other."[15] Bonhoeffer expressed such hope to his fiancée right up to the end. He would write her again anticipating Christmas in 1944. He tucked in the letter a poem, "By Kindly Powers Protected." The last stanza expresses this hope, anchored in his trust in God's omnibenevolence:

By kindly powers so wondrously protected
we wait with confidence, befall what may.
We are with God at night and in the morning,
and, just as certainly, on each new day.[16]

While in Tegel, he would write to her after reading Luke 17:11–17 on the parable of the ten lepers, only one of whom returned to give thanks:

[12] Bonhoeffer to Maria von Wedemeyer, January 17, 1943, *DBWE* 16:384.
[13] Eberhard Bethge, "Postscript," in *Love Letters from Cell 92: The Correspondence between Dietrich Bonhoeffer and Maria von Wedemeyer*, ed. Ruth-Alice von Bismarck and Ulrich Kibitz, trans. John Brownjohn (Nashville: Abingdon, 1995), 365.
[14] Jürgen Moltmann, cited on the *Love Letters* cover.
[15] *Love Letters*, 128.
[16] Ibid., 270.

Dearest Maria,

In all our daily hopes and prayers for a speedy reunion, let us never forget to thank God for all he has given us and continues to give us every day. Then all our thoughts and plans will become clearer and calmer and we shall readily and willingly accept our personal destiny. This week's gospel—about gratitude—is one of those which I love and treasure the most.[17]

He also writes to her of happiness: "You mustn't think I'm unhappy," he says in that same letter from December 19, 1944. "Anyway, what do happiness and unhappiness mean? They depend so little on circumstances and so much more on what goes on inside us. I'm thankful everyday to have you—you and all of you—that makes me happy and cheerful."[18] "I have only to think of you," he wrote on an August day at Tegel, "and all the little shadows on my soul disperse."[19]

They first met at the home of Ruth von Kleist-Retzow, the patroness of the Finkenwalde Seminary and Maria's grandmother. The talk turned to Maria's future plans. She mentioned her desire to study mathematics, which her grandmother took to be "a silly whim." Bonhoeffer, on the other hand, "took it seriously."[20] He was smitten. Bonhoeffer wrote to Bethge of the "delightful memory" of his first meeting with her and the letter proceeds to plot out how to arrange seeing her again.[21] The comment by her grandmother should not be seen as dismissive toward her granddaughter. In fact, Ruth would later be the one trying the hardest to bring the two together.

Those efforts were not so welcome by Maria's mother. Maybe it was due to the age difference, she being exactly half his age at her 18 to his 36. Undeterred, by November 1942, Bonhoeffer requested Maria's mother's permission to ask her daughter to marry him. She consented, but on the condition of a yearlong separation. Bonhoeffer acquiesced. In her diary from November 27, 1942, Maria notes, "The incredible fact remains, he actually wants to marry me."[22] The year of separation never came to be. By the middle of January they were officially engaged. But neither Dietrich nor Maria—nor her mother or grandmother—could foresee the events of April 5, 1943.

Bonhoeffer was sitting at his desk, working. His room, in the attic floor

[17] Ibid., 95. The reference to "This week's gospel" concerns the lectionary reading for that Sunday, Luke 17:11–17.
[18] *Love Letters*, 269.
[19] Ibid., 64.
[20] Ibid., 330.
[21] Bonhoeffer to Eberhard Bethge, June 25, 1942 *DBWE* 16:328–29.
[22] *Love Letters*, 336.

of his parent's home in Charlottenburg, Berlin, was sparsely decorated. Bookshelves lined the wall. His desk was quite plain, having two top-drawers and a lamp perched on top. It was nestled by the radiator and positioned by the window, providing him a view of the tall pines dotting the property. On April 5, 1943, the Gestapo entered the house and arrested him. They had already arrested Dohnanyi and others. The Gestapo traced large financial contributions to Jewish relief agencies. They rightly suspected Bonhoeffer and this circle of involvement in smuggling Jews. But that was only the surface reason for the arrest. The real reason was suspicion for conspiring to assassinate Hitler. Bonhoeffer was taken to Tegel Prison, where he remained until October 1944. Maria visited him as often as she was allowed by the guards. Then Bonhoeffer was moved to the Gestapo prison in Berlin. And here the visits were drastically cut back.

When Maria learned in February 1945 that Bonhoeffer would be transferred from the Gestapo prison in Berlin to Flossenbürg, she went looking for him. She traveled two days by train, then walked over four miles, in the winter, to the entrance to the Flossenbürg Concentration Camp, where she had been told he had been taken. But she was too early. Before Bonhoeffer arrived at Flossenbürg, he was housed at Buchenwald, then briefly at Regensburg. He would not arrive at Flossenbürg until April 8, and would be there for only a day. By then, Maria had long since returned to Berlin and she, as well as the rest of his family, had no idea where he was.

Maria lived with Bonhoeffer's family in Berlin through that spring. As the war ended she borrowed the family car and went looking for her love. In the chaos of the war's end, exacerbated by the Gestapo's destruction of records to avoid incrimination, she could find no trace him and had no idea whether he was alive or dead. Maria would not learn of Bonhoeffer's death until the end of June 1945. Unable to get into Berlin or contact his parents, she could not inform them until the end of July 1945. When she finally did reach them, they mourned his loss together.[23]

After the war, Maria von Wedemeyer studied mathematics at Gottingen University, winning a scholarship for graduate work in the United States, which she completed at Bryn Mawr College in Pennsylvania. She remained in the United States until her death in Massachusetts in 1977.

On August 12, 1943, Dietrich had said to her in a letter:

---

[23] See the historical notes in ibid., 348–59. See also Paul Barz, *I Am Bonhoeffer: A Credible Life, A Novel*, trans. Douglas W. Stott (Minneapolis: Fortress, 2008), 325–39. Though a novel, Barz's book is meticulously researched, including the use of interviews of Maria von Wedemeyer, and well received by Bonhoeffer scholars.

Our marriage shall be a "yes" to God's earth. It must strengthen our resolve to do and to accomplish something on earth. I fear that Christians who venture to stand on earth on only one leg will stand in heaven on only one leg too. . . . So let us continue to be really patient for the rest of the time we're compelled to wait, and not waste a single hour grousing and grumbling. From God's standpoint, this time of waiting is immensely valuable, much depends on how we endure it. . . . I'm convinced that our love and our marriage will derive eternal strength from this time of trial. So let us wait, with and for each other, until our wedding day dawns. It won't be much longer, my dear, dear Maria.[24]

Bethge once referred to the relationship of Dietrich Bonhoeffer to Maria von Wedemeyer as reflective of the "life-affirming theology" Bonhoeffer was "working on" while in prison.[25] We see it so plainly in this letter. His declaration of their marriage as a yes to God's earth is part and parcel of his worldly discipleship. It is a mistake to think of our relationships as outside our spiritual lives. They are every bit the barometer of our love for God. Jonathan Edwards once spoke of his marriage to his wife, Sarah, as an "uncommon union." Bonhoeffer's engagement to Maria von Wedemeyer was of equal stock. In fact, the term *extraordinary* might even be better.

Love Supreme

Bonhoeffer always thought of himself as a pastor, if his last words are any indication. Even Maria's early letters address him as "Pastor Bonhoeffer." The last written words of his to have survived consist of three lines, scribbled inside the cover of his copy of Plutarch's *Lives of Great Men*. The book was a gift from his brother on Dietrich's last birthday, his thirty-ninth, February 6, 1945, and one of the last books his family was able to smuggle into his Berlin prison cell. The next day came the order to move him to Buchenwald. He was not allowed to bring anything with him, including the book. His rough handwriting inside the book suggests that he wrote hurriedly, maybe even anxiously:

Dietrich Bonhoeffer, clergyman
Berlin Charlottenburg
Marienburger Allee 43

---

[24] *Love Letters*, 64–65.
[25] Bethge, "Postscript," in *Love Letters*, 366.

Name, occupation, and address. Note well the occupation, clergyman. Bonhoeffer was ordained on November 15, 1931, at St. Matthew's Church in Berlin. He satisfied the requirements, paid his fee of five reichsmark, and became officially the Reverend Dietrich Bonhoeffer.[26] For a time he served St. Matthew's, which had among its congregants Paul von Hindenburg, president of Germany and former leader of Germany's forces in World War I.[27] Bonhoeffer held various pastoral posts throughout his life, starting with his early post as youth pastor in Barcelona, predating his ordination. He went to Barcelona, he says, to "stand on my own feet," a way of establishing himself as a young man of twenty-two.[28] His pastoral charges and church work would be varied over the next two decades, including pastorates in London and as far away as Harlem, New York City, during his one year of study at Union Theological Seminary, 1929–1930. From his letters during that year, it's clear that Bonhoeffer got far more out of serving at the Abyssinian Baptist Church in Harlem than from his studies at Union.[29] Curiously, his actual pastoral work tended to be more with the youth. With two doctorates, not to mention the ability to play the guitar, he was apparently qualified for such a charge.

Of course, he also was an academic. His career at Berlin was quite short, so he spent most of his time as an educator in the service of the underground church—the apex of which was the seminary at Finkenwalde. Bonhoeffer's mission statement for Finkenwalde, drawn up in 1936, included "intensive preparation for service to others."[30] Bethge informs us that this "was more than an empty phrase."[31] It characterizes his own pastoral ministry and his hopes for the pastors he trained. "Service to others" would become the watchword; the love of neighbor would be the hallmark.

In *Ethics*, Bonhoeffer makes the point, again, of the extraordinary nature of this Christian love: "Love—as understood by the gospel in contrast to all philosophy—is not a method for dealing with people."[32] Love is not some technique; it does not exist in the abstract. Love exists, Bonhoeffer

---

[26] *DBWE* 11:64–65.

[27] In a letter to Paul Lehmann on November 5, 1931, Bonhoeffer writes of Hindenburg: "I think I told you already that it is the church attended by Hindenburg (once a month on average). So I met him personally last Sunday. He seems very discouraged—no wonder, considering the state of things." *DBWE* 11: 62. Hindenburg's Germany was in dire economic straits and on the brink of falling apart.

[28] Bonhoeffer, "Spanish Diary," January–March 1928, *DBWE* 10:57.

[29] Metaxas sees Bonhoeffer's ministry in Harlem as a turning point in his life, noting, "For the first time Bonhoeffer saw the gospel preached and lived out in obedience to God's commands." Eric Metaxas, *Bonhoeffer: Pastor, Martyr, Prophet, Spy* (Nashville: Thomas Nelson, 2010), 108.

[30] Cited in Eberhard Bethge, *Dietrich Bonhoeffer: A Biography*, enl. ed. (Minneapolis: Fortress, 2000), 539.

[31] Ibid.

[32] *DBWE* 6:241.

continues, "in God's actual loving of human beings and the world," and so our love exists "only as a real belonging-together and being-together of people with other human beings and with the world."[33] As he did in *The Cost of Discipleship*, Bonhoeffer brings us to the Sermon on the Mount: "The Sermon on the Mount as the proclamation of the incarnate love of God calls people to love one another, and thus to reject everything that hinders fulfilling this task—in short, it calls them to self-denial."[34]

Bonhoeffer goes on to explain what self-denial fully entails while also laying out for us what self-denial opens us to experience. In short, all along we suffer from a faulty perception of what's best for us. Self-promotion, self-service, self-focus all leave us shriveled up and hollow. As a result, we can't see properly. Bonhoeffer explains:

> In renouncing one's own happiness, one's own rights, one's own righteousness, one's own dignity, in renouncing violence and success, in renouncing one's own life, a person is prepared to love one's neighbor. God's love liberates human perception, which has been clouded and led astray by love of self, for the clear recognition of reality, of the neighbor, and of the world.[35]

Bonhoeffer learned firsthand all that self-denial entails. But he also learned firsthand all that such self-denial opened to him. He could revel in God's love in Christ, even during the long, dark night he experienced.

In 1965, John Coltrane, America's great jazz musician, released the album *A Love Supreme*. It represents, as music critics attest, not only Coltrane's musical highpoint, but equally the apex of his spiritual quest and his aim to offer, accordingly, a musical tribute to God. Leading up to the recording of the album, Coltrane explored as many religious sources as he could find in his attempt to understand love. In the end, the resolution to his quest eluded him. And while the studio sessions recorded one fine album, maybe the best of American jazz, the album stops short of achieving its goal.[36]

Bonhoeffer reminds us that understanding love does not mean tracing out every path to the feet of a guru—our modern-day Christian gurus

---

[33] *DBWE* 6:241.
[34] *DBWE* 6:242.
[35] *DBWE* 6:242.
[36] See Ashley Kahn, *A Love Supreme: The Story of John Coltrane's Signature Album* (New York: Penguin, 2003).

included. To understand and then to live in light of a love supreme, we need only to look to the incarnate Christ, to see his call to love one another, to love our neighbor, to love our enemy. That is an "extraordinary" love, a love supreme.

In bringing our discussion to Bonhoeffer on the Christian life to an end, I am conscious of the irony of my using Bonhoeffer as a model for us, myself included, all the while stressing that we follow Christ alone and look to Christ alone.

Allow me one more ironic indulgence: that is to say that Bonhoeffer's maturity is startling. Not only does he have many of his key ideas in place before he takes his doctorate at twenty-one years of age, but he's already publishing them. In addition to his rapid intellectual and theological maturity is his extensive awareness of the world and rich experience of it as a rather young man. In April–May 1924, Bonhoeffer toured Italy—the "Grand Tour" was a requisite of European children of means—as well as North Africa, and he kept a diary. In Rome, the Colosseum, the Forum, and St. Peter's all overwhelmed him. But he was particularly struck by the *Laocoön*. This marble statue, made in the first century BC, was lost and then discovered in 1506—Michelangelo was on hand for the unearthing—and was eventually housed in the Vatican Museums. There Bonhoeffer saw it and recorded in his diary, "When I saw the Laocoön there for the first time, a chill actually went through me. It is unbelievable. I spent a lot of time there."[37]

The story of Laocoön comes to us from Greek mythology. He was the priest at Troy who vainly attempted to warn the Trojans not to accept the Trojan Horse: "Beware of Greeks bearing gifts." He met his end by two serpents, called forth by Poseidon in judgment. The statue depicts Laocoön's anguished face as the serpents entangle him. Struggling but powerless, Laocoön proves no match for his fate. It is a moving and compelling statue. Bonhoeffer was quite right to afford it pride of place among the artistic wonders of Rome.

But as a recently turned eighteen-year-old, Bonhoeffer could not quite see *Laocoön* deeply enough. That would come later. In 1942, he found himself back in Italy, Mussolini's Italy. He was accompanying his brother-in-law Hans von Dohnanyi, the latter engaged in *Abwehr* affairs. It's not entirely clear what Bonhoeffer was doing, but whatever it was it did not demand much of his time. That he spent revisiting the sites, museums, and

---

[37] Bonhoeffer, "Italian Diary," April 14, 1924, *DBWE* 9:89.

galleries. And, of course, he went to see the *Laocoön*. On his list of "Main Impressions," *Laocoön* again takes first place. This time, however, Bonhoeffer notches up his respect: "Did the head of Laocoön become some sort of model for later portrayals of Christ? The ancient 'man of sorrows.' No one was able to inform me about this; will attempt to investigate it."[38]

In a way, this typifies how we all, Bonhoeffer included, mature in our Christian life. More and more we see Christ. More and more we trace our experiences, our lives, back to Christ. More and more we live through, in, and toward Christ. Bonhoeffer once observed, in *Ethics*, "Knowledge of reality is not just knowing external events, but seeing into the essence of things."[39]

Little wonder Bonhoeffer saw in the anguished face, in the struggle with a serpent, Christ. It is in Christ's suffering, as the Man of Sorrows, that we meet him, that we come to him. And it is in knowing that Christ suffered that we take comfort. Of course, unlike the serpents attacking Laocoön, the biblical Serpent could only bruise Christ's heel. Christ, however, crushed his head. This is the essence of things.

Conclusion: Christotelic Discipleship

This story in marble of the *Laocoön* highlights for us the three key components of Christ: his incarnation, his crucifixion, and his resurrection. These doctrines course through Bonhoeffer's writings. He says, "In Jesus Christ we believe in the God who became human, crucified, resurrected God. In the incarnation we recognize God's love for creation, in the crucifixion God's judgment over all flesh, and in the resurrection, God's will to a new world."[40] Each of these doctrines needs a closer look.

Incarnation

In his incarnation, Christ as the God-man shouts *yes* to us and to God's earth—just as Bonhoeffer's marriage would be an echo of that yes. When we live in the world in love, reflecting Christ, we too, echo that yes. We see this brought into sharp focus in a lecture from November 19, 1932. Bonhoeffer titled the lecture, which he delivered to the Protestant Continuing Education Institute for Women, "Thy Kingdom Come: The Prayer of the Church-

---

[38] July 16, 1942, *DBWE* 16:402. Bonhoeffer's diary fragments of 1942, of which this was a part, contain embellishments intended for the Gestapo. He did, in fact, visit Rome July 3–10 and spent the next week, including the 16th, in Germany.
[39] *DBWE* 6:81.
[40] *DBWE* 6:157.

Community for God's Kingdom on Earth."[41] In the lecture, Bonhoeffer acknowledges, "We live on cursed ground that yields thorns and thistles." Then he declares, "But—Christ has entered into this cursed earth; the flesh Christ bore was taken from this ground."[42] Bonhoeffer notes how the church too is firmly planted on this cursed ground: "God plants his kingdom in the cursed ground."[43] And this is where God calls us to live for him.

Bonhoeffer ends the lecture by turning to the curious episode of Jacob's wrestling with an angel (Gen. 32:22–29). Bonhoeffer sees in it a fitting description of our living in the world:

> For all of us the way into the promised land [the new heaven and the new earth] passes through the night, that we too only enter it as those strangely marked with scars from the struggle with God, the struggle for God's kingdom and grace; that we enter into the land of God and of our brother as limping warriors.[44]

His image of us as "limping warriors" helps us cultivate some of that humility and dependence upon God we so desperately need.

In one of his last letters to Bethge, Bonhoeffer writes, "If this earth was good enough for the man Jesus Christ, if such a man as Jesus lived, then, and only then, life has a meaning for us."[45] As Christ came into this earth, not hovering six inches off the ground, but fully *here*, so too we are called to live for Christ in this world. "This world," Bonhoeffer writes from a prison cell and with Hitler at the helm of his country, "cannot be prematurely written off."[46]

We also see in the incarnation the humility of Christ. He came as and among the poor and the outcast, the exiles, the "occupied." In all of these Bonhoeffer could find both comfort and challenge. To live through, in, and toward Christ means to live from the perspective of and the model of the incarnation.

Crucifixion

It also means to live from, and by, the crucifixion. While we know the ground is cursed, the crucifixion reveals the utter depths, ugliness, and ter-

---

[41] *DBWE* 12:285–97, see editor's note , page 285n1.
[42] *DBWE* 12:288.
[43] *DBWE* 12:295.
[44] *DBWE* 12:297. See also Bonhoeffer's sermon on Jacob's wrestling with God, in *DBWE* 11:428–33.
[45] Bonhoeffer to Eberhard Bethge, August 21, 1944, *LPP*, 391.
[46] Bonhoeffer to Eberhard Bethge, June 27, 1944, *LPP*, 337.

ror of sin and evil. The crucifixion also underscores true humility marked by love. God so loved the world that he sent his Son not only into the world, but to the cross. In the process, Christ "becomes the one upon whom ultimately all human guilt falls. Jesus does not shirk it but bears it in humility and infinite love."[47] Bonhoeffer adds, "Out of his selfless love for human beings, out of his sinlessness, Jesus enters into human guilt, taking it upon himself."[48] We stand, forgiven, justified, redeemed, and reconciled as a result. We have peace with God (Rom. 5:1–5).

We are also brought into the church-community as a result of Christ's death on the cross—a community of the forgiven, who should be quick to forgive, a community of those who have been interceded for and should be, likewise, quick to intercede, and a community whose burdens have been lifted and who should be quick to bear the burdens of others. Bonhoeffer sees the church as the church under the cross. We see ourselves as poor sinners in need of grace, just as we see our fellow human beings as poor sinners in need of grace. As we saw earlier, Bonhoeffer once said, "A King who dies on the cross must be the King of a rather strange kingdom."[49] The church is a strange, or rather "extraordinary," kingdom.

Resurrection

And then we come to the resurrection. Living the Christian life in, through, and toward Christ, means living in light of the resurrection. This gives us one word to ponder: *hope.*

Bonhoeffer wrote, while in prison, that it is "certainly not a mere conventional dictum, that man cannot live without hope," adding, "for a Christian there must be hope based on a firm foundation. . . . How great a power there is in a hope that is based on certainty, and how invincible a life with such a hope is."[50] Then Bonhoeffer declares, "'Christ our hope'—this Pauline formula is the strength of our lives."[51]

Recalling the sermon on Matthew 2 and the incident of Herod's slaughter of the innocents, we remember how Bonhoeffer confronted head-on the ugly realities of the sin-cursed world. But at the end of that sermon he points us to the resolution of suffering and the resolution of the perplexities of life.

---

[47] *DBWE* 6:234.
[48] *DBWE* 6:234.
[49] Bonhoeffer, "The Essence of Christianity," December 11, 1928, *DBWE* 10:357.
[50] Bonhoeffer to Eberhard Bethge, July 25, 1944, *LPP*, 372–73.
[51] Ibid., 373.

Twice Bonhoeffer proclaims, "Jesus lives."[52] Jesus lives, therefore we have hope. In *Ethics*, Bonhoeffer announces, "Jesus Christ—the resurrected—that means that God, in love and omnipotence, makes an end of death, and calls a new creation into life. God gives new life."[53] We have hope.

Following Christ means following the incarnate, crucified, risen Christ. We have a tendency to focus on one of these at the expense of the other two. Sometimes models of the Christian life privilege one over the other two. If all we have is the incarnate Christ, then we end up with moralism. If we simply see the crucifixion, then we have asceticism. And if all we focus on is the resurrection, then we have a view that simply doesn't resonate with the "minor key" moments of life. By focusing on one of these exclusively we end up with a warped view of the Christian life. We must hold on to the complexity of Christ as he comes to us in Scripture. We need to remember all three of these as we seek to follow Christ.

Bonhoeffer makes the case that when we have faith in the incarnate, crucified, and risen Christ, which God gifts to us, along with it comes love and hope. This is life in Christ—the life of faith, love, and hope because of Christ. Bonhoeffer calls this *Christusleben*, the life-in-Christ.[54] And in this we are truly alive. "So heaven is torn open above us humans, and the joyful message of God's salvation in Jesus Christ rings out from heaven to earth as a cry of joy. I believe, and in believing I receive Christ, I have everything. I live before God."[55]

---

[52] Bonhoeffer, sermon on Matt. 2:13–23, January 1, 1940, *DBWE* 15: 494.
[53] *DBWE* 6:158.
[54] *DBWE* 6:149.
[55] *DBWE* 6:148.

PART 5

LITERATURE

I would like to ask you to take complete control of my things. I'm told that even a dinner jacket would be accepted; please give mine away. . . . In short, give away whatever anyone might need, and don't give it another thought. . . . Now for a few more requests: unfortunately there were no books handed in here for me today; Commissar Sonderegger would be willing to accept them every now and then if Maria could bring them. I should be very grateful for them. . . . Could I please have some tooth paste and a few coffee beans? Father, could you get me from the library Lienhard and Abendstunden eines Einsiedlers *by H. Pestalozzi, So-zialpädagogik by P. Natorp, and Plutarch's* Lives of Great Men?[1] *I'm getting on all right. Do keep well. Many thanks for everything.*

With all my heart, your grateful Dietrich

Please leave some writing paper with the Commissar!

DIETRICH BONHOEFFER TO HIS PARENTS, FROM PRINZ-ALBRECHT-STRASSE,[2] BERLIN, 1945 (BONHOEFFER'S LAST LETTER)

---

[1] Of these books, only Plutarch's *Lives* was delivered. He wrote his name and address in it and left it behind in his cell at Prinz-Albrecht-Strasse before being moved on to Buchenwald and then to Flossenbürg. Somehow, amid all the chaos in Berlin, the book made its way back to Bonhoeffer's family.
[2] This served as Gestapo headquarters. Bonhoeffer was imprisoned in the dungeon in the cellar.

CHAPTER 10

READING BONHOEFFER

A student who doesn't want his work to go for nothing ought to read and reread some good author until the author becomes part, as it were, of his flesh and blood.

MARTIN LUTHER, *TABLE TALK*, 1533

I did make a dutiful attempt to read his books, starting from the beginning with Sanctorum Communio. *When I admitted my frustration it amused him thoroughly. He claimed that the only one of concern to him at the moment was* Life Together, *and he preferred that I wait until he was around to read it.*

MARIA VON WEDEMEYER

There are any number of photographs of Bonhoeffer that are intriguing. The one with him seated by his twin sister, Sabine, in the backyard of her London townhome on the eve of World War II, or the one of him in the courtyard at Tegel Prison, with sleeves rolled up and a book in his hand, or the one of him playing Ping-Pong, presumably against a not-so-worthy opponent as one hand holds the paddle and the other rests in his suit pocket—all of these photos draw us to Bonhoeffer. But the one I am coming to appreciate more and more is one of the many photographs of him on the beach. With hands clasped around bended knees, Bonhoeffer sits surrounded by students. One of the students, an "unidentified Swede," has open notebook and pen in hand. The others, Germans all, listen intently.

Bonhoeffer holds forth. One of those students, Inge Karding, later recalls, "From the very beginning, he taught us that we had to read the Bible as it was directed at us, as the word of God directly to us."[1]

I suppose I'm drawn to this particular picture because I am a teacher and, though personally too many miles away from a beach to pull this off, I see this as representing the ideal of my profession. I'm also drawn to this picture because I would so enjoy sitting and listening to Bonhoeffer, and especially at the beach. The next best thing, however, is reading him.

Eberhard Bethge knew what it was like to spend time with Bonhoeffer. When they were separated by their respective Nazi prisons, they still managed to spend time together through the written word. In one letter, Bethge says, "When my thoughts have crystallized too rigidly, you come along and stir them up each time so they appear in a new constellation and once again offer the observant eye new, pleasant, or exciting aspects for some time to come."[2]

We'll look at Bonhoeffer's ability to stir things up in books by him and also in books about him.

Books by Bonhoeffer: A Place to Start

Bonhoeffer's *Life Together* is likely the best place to start reading him. This short book is both packed and rather challenging. Next I would recommend *Letters and Papers from Prison*. While this book could be read straight through, and such a reading well repays itself, dipping in this book from time to time tends to nourish well. The third book is *The Collected Sermons of Dietrich Bonhoeffer*. This offers thirty-one of the sermon manuscripts from Bonhoeffer's writings. Then comes *The Cost of Discipleship*. There's a reason this book is a classic, as we have seen. To return to a slimmer volume, *Meditations on the Cross* offers insightful readings from across the spectrum and the decades of Bonhoeffer's writings. A bonus to this top-five list is his unfinished magnum opus, *Ethics*. Be warned, though, this is a book sometimes best digested a paragraph at a time. On sheer level of difficulty this hovers near a 10, but is essential to understanding Bonhoeffer's main ideas. So here's the list of the top five, with a bonus:

---

[1] Inge Karding, an interview with Martin Doblmeier, cited in Eric Metaxas, *Bonhoeffer: Pastor, Martyr, Prophet, Spy* (Nashville: Thomas Nelson, 2010), 129.
[2] Eberhard Bethge to Bonhoeffer, September 21, 1944, *DBWE* 8:541.

Life Together. Available in two English editions: Translated by Jon W. Doberstein. San Francisco: HarperOne, 1954, 1978; *DBWE* 5, *Life Together* and *Prayerbook of the Bible*. Minneapolis: Fortress, 1996.

Letters and Papers from Prison. Edited by Eberhard Bethge. New York: Simon & Schuster, 1997.

The Collected Sermons of Dietrich Bonhoeffer. Edited by Isabel Best. Minneapolis: Fortress, 2012.

The Cost of Discipleship. Available in two English editions: Translated by R. H. Fuller. New York: Simon & Schuster, 1995; *DBWE* 4, *Discipleship*. Minneapolis: Fortress, 2001.

Meditations on the Cross. Edited by Manfred Weber. Translated by Douglas W. Stott. Louisville: Westminster John Knox, 1998.

And the bonus, for the stout of heart:

Ethics. Available in two English editions: Translated by Neville Horton Smith. New York: Simon & Schuster, 1995; *DBWE* 6, *Ethics*. Minneapolis: Fortress, 2005.

Books by Bonhoeffer: Continuing the Journey

After these six, next would be *A Year with Dietrich Bonhoeffer: Daily Meditations from His Letters, Writings, and Sermons*, edited by Carla Barnhill (San Francisco: HarperOne, 2005). Worthy also is *Dietrich Bonhoeffer's Christmas Sermons*, edited by Edwin H. Robertson (Grand Rapids: Zondervan, 2005). Finally, the little reader *Reflections on the Bible: Human Word and Word of God*, edited by Manfred Weber and translated by Eugene M. Boring (Peabody, MA: Hendrickson, 2002), is quite helpful for a variety of texts on Bonhoeffer's doctrine of Scripture.

A helpful and rather large reader that pulls from the variety of Bonhoeffer's writings is *A Testament to Freedom: The Essential Writings of Dietrich Bonhoeffer*, edited by Geffrey B. Kelly and F. Burton Nelson (San Francisco: HarperOne, 1995).

The next step for the diehards would be to start reading through the set of Bonhoeffer's writings, the sixteen-volume *Dietrich Bonhoeffer Works*, published in English by Fortress Press. These are the scholarly editions of Bonhoeffer's writings, complete with introductory essays, copious notes, and helpful end matter, including a chronology of events and writings of the volume, a full bibliography, and an index of names that includes brief

LITERATURE

descriptions of the people mentioned in the volume. All but one volume are available, with volume 14, *Theological Education at Finkenwalde: 1935–1937*, forthcoming. Then for the Truly Committed: learn German, if you don't know it already, and tackle the source, the sixteen-volume *Dietrich Bonhoeffer Werke*.

I will also offer one out-of-print recommendation. The *Letters and Papers from Prison* volume does not contain all of Bonhoeffer's letters, namely, all of the letters passing between him and his fiancée, Maria von Wedemeyer. To read those, find the rare *Love Letters from Cell 92: The Correspondence between Dietrich Bonhoeffer and Maria von Wedemeyer, 1943–45*, edited by Ruth-Alice von Bismarck and Ulrich Kabitz (Nashville: Abingdon, 1995).

Books about Bonhoeffer: A Place to Start

A book that is a delight to read as well as to simply flip through and keep on the coffee table is *Dietrich Bonhoeffer: A Life in Pictures*, edited by Renate Bethge and Christian Gremmels. Mrs. Bethge is Bonhoeffer's niece who married Eberhard Bethge. In this book, text and pictures combine to give an intimate look at Bonhoeffer's life. Next I would recommend Eric Metaxas's *Bonhoeffer: Pastor, Martyr, Prophet, Spy*. Crisply written, this book walks us through his life. It is virtually impossible not to come away from Metaxas's book unaffected and unchallenged. Another way to get at Bonhoeffer's life is Paul Barz's *I Am Bonhoeffer: A Credible Life*. This is a novel, but masterfully researched and esteemed highly by Bonhoeffer scholars. His discussion of what happened to Maria von Wedemeyer after Bonhoeffer's death is moving. Next would be *Dietrich Bonhoeffer 1906–1945: Martyr, Thinker, Man of Resistance*, by Ferdinand Schlingensiepen. The Bonhoeffer guild likes this biography more than Metaxas's, but it doesn't quite read with the same energy.

Finally, there is the slightly over one-thousand-page biography by Eberhard Bethge. If you have a great deal of time on your hands, this is the book for you. It provides a nearly month-by-month detailed chronicle of Bonhoeffer's life by his former student at Finkenwalde, his main correspondent during the imprisonment, and the husband of his aforementioned niece. Bethge devoted an entire career to overseeing the literary legacy of Bonhoeffer. Bethge's biography is his own legacy. It's giant, but gripping and most rewarding. This is the Mount Everest of biographies.

So here is the top-five list:

Dietrich Bonhoeffer: A Life in Pictures. Edited by Renate Bethge and Christian Gremmels. Minneapolis: Fortress, 2005.

Metaxas, Eric. *Bonhoeffer: Pastor, Martyr, Prophet, Spy.* Nashville: Thomas Nelson, 2010.

Barz, Paul. *I Am Bonhoeffer: A Credible Life, A Novel.* Minneapolis: Fortress, 2006.

Schlingensiepen, Ferdinand. *Dietrich Bonhoeffer 1906–1945: Martyr, Thinker, Man of Resistance.* London: T&T Clark, 2011.

Bethge, Eberhard. *Dietrich Bonhoeffer: A Biography*, Enlarged edition. Minneapolis: Fortress, 2000.

Books about Bonhoeffer: Continuing the Journey

Martin Marty has contributed a delightful book in his *Dietrich Bonhoeffer's "Letters and Papers from Prison": A Biography* (Princeton University Press, 2011), part of the cleverly designed series Lives of Religious Books. For a more comprehensive look at Bonhoeffer's thought, Sabine Dramm's *Dietrich Bonhoeffer: An Introduction to His Thought* (Grand Rapids: Baker Academic: 2007) is quite helpful. Craig J. Slane looks at Bonhoeffer's life and controversial engagement in the assassination plots, especially using the lens of the Finkenwalde experience, in *Bonhoeffer as Martyr: Social Responsibility and Modern Christian Commitment* (Grand Rapids: Brazos, 2004). Though a slim book, John W. Matthews's *Anxious Souls Will Ask: The Christ-Centered Spirituality of Dietrich Bonhoeffer* (Grand Rapids: Eerdmans, 2005) helps us understand Bonhoeffer's prophetic life, which in turn challenges us to take our prophetic stand in our culture. Mark Devine's *Bonhoeffer Speaks Today: Following Jesus at All Costs* (Nashville: Broadman & Holman, 2005) is a nicely written application of Bonhoeffer's life to church life today. Rounding out these books would be the very helpful collection of essays edited by Keith L. Johnson and Timothy Larsen, *Bonhoeffer, Christ and Culture* (Downers Grove, IL: IVP Academic, 2013). These essays, from the Wheaton Theology Conference, explore his theology and legacy.

I will also offer one out-of-print recommendation, that of Wolf-Dieter Zimmermann and Ronald Gregor Smith, *I Knew Dietrich Bonhoeffer* (San Francisco: Harper & Row, 1966). This collection of remembrances of Bonhoeffer by former students, associates, and relatives further pulls the curtain back on his life and thought.

Wait for the Movie

In addition to these books, you can also spend time with Bonhoeffer on film. Martin Doblmeier produced a feature-length documentary for the centenary of Bonhoeffer's birth, *Bonhoeffer* (Journey Films, 2006). Other documentaries include *Hanged on a Twisted Cross: The Life, Convictions, and Martyrdom of Dietrich Bonhoeffer*, by T. N. Mohan and narrated by Ed Asner (Lathika International Film, 1996), and *Dietrich Bonhoeffer: Memories and Perspectives* (Vision Video/Trinity Films, 1983). In addition to these documentaries, there is also the movie *Bonhoeffer: Agent of Grace* (Vision Video, 2000).

Desert-Island Top Five

Life Together
The Collected Sermons of Dietrich Bonhoeffer
Ethics
Dietrich Bonhoeffer: A Life in Pictures
Bonhoeffer: Pastor, Martyr, Prophet, Spy

Please don't ever get anxious or worried about me, but don't forget to pray for me—I'm sure you don't. I am so sure of God's guiding hand that I hope I shall always be kept in that certainty. You must never doubt that I'm traveling with gratitude and cheerfulness along the road where I'm being led. My past life is brim-full of God's goodness, and my sins are covered by the forgiving love of Christ crucified. I'm most thankful for the people I have met, and I only hope that they never have to grieve about me, but that they, too, will always be certain of, and thankful for, God's mercy and forgiveness. (Dietrich Bonhoeffer, Tegel Prison, August 23, 1944)

A TIME LINE OF
BONHOEFFER'S LIFE

1906	Born, February 6, Berlin
1923–1924	Theological studies, Tübingen, Berlin; travels to Italy and North Africa
1927	Takes first doctorate; writes *Sanctorum Communio*
1928	Ministry in Barcelona
1930	Takes second doctorate; qualifies as university professor; writes *Act and Being*
1930–1931	Studies at Union Theological Seminary, New York; ministry in Harlem; extensive travels across United States and to Cuba
1931–1932	Lectures at the University of Berlin, including his lectures on Christ (published posthumously from student notes as *Christ the Center*) and his lectures *Creation and Fall* (published in 1933)
1933	Early work in the Confessing Church; writes early draft and August Version of the Bethel Confession; begins London ministry in October
1934	Returns from London in the spring for his work among the ecumenical movement; attends the Fanø conference in August; briefly returns to London in November
1935	Opens preacher's seminary, underground seminary for the Confessing Church first in Zingst, then at Finkenwalde
1936	License to teach at the University of Berlin revoked by the Gestapo; continues lectures and work at Finkenwalde; publishes *The Cost of Discipleship*
1937	Gestapo closes Finkenwalde, twenty-seven students arrested; Bonhoeffer begins work with collective pastorates in the region of Pomerania

1938	Writes *Life Together*; continues work with collective pastorates
1939	Leaves for the United States; decides to return; continues work with collective pastorates
1940	Gestapo closes collective pastorate sites at Koslin and Sighurdsof; Bonhoeffer encouraged by his brother-in-law Hans von Dohnanyi to join the *Abwehr* (military intelligence); forbidden by Gestapo to "speak in public" or write; begins writing *Ethics*
1941	Travels extensively for the *Abwehr* and works for the Confessing Church; works on *Ethics*; reports on "Operation 7," the Deportation of the Jews from Berlin and other cities
1942	Travels extensively for the *Abwehr* and works for Confessing Church; meets Maria von Wedemeyer and in November seeks engagement with her
1943	Becomes engaged in January; arrested by Gestapo and put in Tegel Prison, April 5; begins prison writings (letters, poems, fiction, and continues to work on *Ethics*)
1944	Sits in Tegel Prison, awaiting trial, continues prison writings; July 20 Valkyrie Plot fails; Zossen files discovered in September; Bonhoeffer moved to Berlin, to cellar dungeon of Gestapo headquarters, Prinz-Albrecht-Strasse, there writing significantly curtailed
1945	February 7 (day after thirty-ninth birthday) moved to Buchenwald, then Regensburg; April 5 Hitler issues execution order; April 8, Bonhoeffer moved to Flossenbürg; hanged, Flossenbürg Concentration Camp, April 9[1]

---

[1] For detailed timelines, see the appendices in the *Dietrich Bonhoeffer Works* volumes, which include the chronology related to the time period covered in each volume.

SUMMARY OF BONHOEFFER ON THE CHRISTIAN LIFE

In Christ
Doctrine of Christ

Christotelic Discipleship:
Living in and toward the Incarnate,
Crucified, and Risen Lord

Incarnation
• cultivating humility and dependence
• "this-worldly discipleship"

Crucifixion
• living under and from the cross
• being forgiven and giving forgiveness
• living in God's grace, mercy, and love
• understanding and embracing suffering

Resurrection
• "Jesus is alive. I have hope."
• risen with Christ

From the Cross

In Community
Doctrine of the Church

The Church-Community

Prayer
• alone
• together, bearing one another's burden

Scripture
• preaching and proclamation of the Word
• reading, obeying, and living the Word

Confession
• teaching and wrestling with theology
• living theologically

Sacraments
• baptism and the Lord's Supper as nourishment for life, as the means of grace

In Love
Ethics

Following Christ

Loving the Triune God

Loving Our Neighbor/Living in the World

Dying to Self, Being Risen with Christ

Freedom from Slavery to Self,
Freedom to Serve Others

As We Live in the World . . .
"The Four Mandates"
• work
• marriage
• government
• church

For the World

GENERAL INDEX

Abbot, Shirley, 58
Abwehr, 163, 164, 178
Abyssinian Baptist Church (Harlem), 50, 176
activism, of evangelicalism, 82
Adam, historicity of, 87n15
alien righteousness, 36, 41, 138
already/not yet, 142
Altizer, Thomas J. J., 80n1
America, Bonhoeffer on, 50
Apostles' Creed, 105, 118
architecture, 22
art, 22
Aryan race, 32–33, 35
asceticism, 182
Augsburg Confession, 119
Augustine, 80, 170
authenticity, 25, 73

Babcock, Maltbie, 135
Barker, William S., 121
Barmen Declaration, 44, 46
Barnhill, Carla, 187
Barth, Karl, 80, 87n15, 101–2, 121, 137
Barz, Paul, 174n23, 188, 189
bearing, 70, 71, 159
Beatitudes, 169
Bebbington, David, 82
Berlin
  Gestapo prison in, 22, 24, 174, 175
  Olympics (1936), 33
  student days at, 23–24, 60
  teaching post in, 19, 27, 47, 176

Bethel, Germany, 43–44, 48, 63
Bethel Confession, 49, 85–86, 88, 91
Bethge, Eberhard, 23, 33n4, 42, 63–64, 65, 90–91, 120, 137, 138, 144, 152, 172, 175, 176, 186, 187, 188, 189
Bethge, Renate, 188, 189
Bible
  authority of, 87–89
  obedience to, 96–97
  submission to, 95–96
  as Word of God, 82–83, 87
Bible reading, 92–98
biblicism, 66–67, 82
Bismarck, Ruth-Alice von, 188
Bonhoeffer, Dietrich
  as academic, 176
  care for family members, 171
  courage and heroism of, 51–52
  criticism of liberalism, 88–89
  death of, 27, 154, 164
  ecumenical efforts of, 80
  imprisonment of, 134, 171
  as liberal, 79–80
  as Lutheran, 25
  as martyr, 22, 164–65
  maturity of, 178–79
  as pastor, 175–76
  as poet, 157
  return to Germany, 20
  as spy, 22, 163–64
  suffering of, 153
  as theological conservative, 79–82, 83

SCRIPTURE INDEX

GAINING WISDOM FROM THE PAST FOR LIFE IN THE PRESENT

Other volumes in the Theologians on the Christian Life series

FRED G. ZASPEL

WARFIELD
on the Christian Life

LIVING IN LIGHT OF THE GOSPEL

Now Available

WILLIAM EDGAR

SCHAEFFER
on the Christian Life

COUNTERCULTURAL SPIRITUALITY

Now Available

FRED SANDERS

WESLEY
on the Christian Life

THE HEART RENEWED IN LOVE

August 2013

Visit crossway.org for more information.